The Faber Book of MODERN EUROPEAN POETRY

The Faber Book of

MODERN EUROPEAN POETRY

Edited by A. Alvarez

faber and faber

LONDON · BOSTON

First published in 1992
by Faber and Faber Limited
3 Queen Square London WC1N 3AU

Photoset by Wilmaset Ltd, Wirral
Printed in England by Clays Ltd, St Ives plc

A CIP record for this book
is available from the British Library

ISBN 0–571–14321–0

10 9 8 7 6 5 4 3 2 1

CONTENTS

RUSSIA

INTRODUCTION

Until quite recently, foreign literature, particularly foreign poetry, has not fared well in Britain. I discovered this for myself back in 1965 when Penguin brought me in to beef up their series of Modern European Poets in Translation. Although this series published some of the best and most exciting poetry that was appearing at that time – the first three volumes under my editorship were Miroslav Holub, Zbigniew Herbert and Vasko Popa – the books were scarcely noticed. The series ran for twelve years and included a further twenty-two volumes, but they were reviewed hardly at all and sold badly, until the accountants finally decided enough was enough. In the circumstances, they were probably justified. With rare exceptions, of course, the audience for contemporary poetry is always small and specialized. But in those days, when Larkin's ironic form of Englishness was producing paroxysms of Little Englishism in his admirers, no one had much time for the poetry of foreigners. If they bothered with an excuse – mostly, they didn't – it was the old chestnut: poetry is what gets lost in translation.

Maybe it is. For example, I am told that, for his fellow countrymen, part of Zbigniew Herbert's originality and influence resides in the way he has transformed the language and technique of Polish poetry. None of that survives translation – or is even translatable. But that does not make his poems any less extraordinary when you read him in English. They have a strength and range and independence and restraint – to use an unfashionable word, a nobility – that to my mind makes them, *even in translation*, better than most poems written in English in the last quarter of a century. Similarly, Miroslav Holub's poems are idiomatic, translucent and sane in a way that makes you feel they would work powerfully in any language. I hope this anthology will show that there are a number of poets whose work is so strong that, no matter what subtleties are lost in translation, it emerges from the process as poetry in its own right.

The reverse is also true, alas. There are many important poets whose work does not jump the language barrier so effectively. No matter how good the translation, the reader knows that something vital has been lost and what he is getting is an approximation, a

black-and-white reproduction of the original oil painting. Celan is
the obvious example, despite Michael Hamburger's brilliant, scrupu-
lous work. But Celan's poetry, as Hamburger says, is also enor-
mously difficult in the original German. He was pushing at the limits
of language, probing its subatomic structure, breaking it down and
reconstructing it for his own purposes. The reader has to be aware of
the etymological roots of the words and must pick up arcane literary
echoes and personal references in order to understand properly all
the resonances of the poems. It is a formidable task for those who
speak German, almost impossible for those who don't.

Celan, however, is an extreme case. In general, when the first
modernists jettisoned traditional metre and rhyme and poetic
diction in favour of less predictable forms and a language closer to
colloquial speech a good deal of contemporary poetry became easier
to translate. In place of the brilliant anomalies which had previously
been regarded as masterpieces of translation – such as Gilbert
Murray's transformation of Aeschylus into Swinburne – a new
system evolved: poets collaborated with people who knew the
original language to produce accurate translations that also read like
English poems.

Clearly, the system worked best with free verse, which may be
why modern Russian poetry has had such a hard time in English. I
do not know Russian so I cannot say whether even the best
twentieth-century Russian poets – Mandelstam, Pasternak, Tsve-
taeva and Ahkmatova – tended to stick to relatively traditional
forms because what Nabokov called 'my untrammelled, rich and
infinitely docile Russian tongue' runs naturally to sonorities, regular
rhythm and regular rhyme, or because the profoundly middlebrow
preferences of the cultural commissars were harder to buck than
those of the cultural commissars in the West. Whatever the reason,
their work seems to reach us more veiled and remote and with more
of its essence missing than that of many of the major poets in other
European languages. The same is true of contemporary Spanish
poetry, which mostly seems lame and inflated in English. The more a
poet relies on the traditional rhymed and metrically regular forms,
the more his weaknesses are exaggerated and his strengths are
concealed in translation. I imagine Yeats's marvellous poems would
present similar problems in a foreign language, whereas Eliot,
despite his extraordinary ear for the movement and inner rhythm of

verse, seems to have survived translations without major difficulties. (Jaroslav Seifert, the Czech equivalent of Yeats, is much loved by his compatriots for his power and vitality, neither of which comes across in translation.)

In England, however, foreign poetry was dismissed not simply because of the problems, or impossibility, of translation. The studied indifference of the Little Englanders to foreign poetry was part of their distaste for Modernism itself, which was, from the start, both American-led and closely tied to continental literature. The prime movers – Pound, Eliot, Stevens – unlike their British contemporaries, were not constrained by the long tradition of English verse stretching back to Chaucer. They felt free to pick and choose from world literature, and this eclectic cosmopolitanism was, for them, a source of great energy. Writing of Yeats, the last of the great traditionalists, Eliot said: 'The kind of poetry that I needed, to teach me the use of my own voice, did not exist in English at all; it was only to be found in French.' When Eliot wrote his essay 'The Metaphysical Poets' he praised Donne and his followers for qualities he admired in Laforgue and Corbière. Similarly, Pound, whose whole oeuvre is stuffed, magpie-fashion, with glittering bits and pieces from foreign and ancient literatures, first found his true voice through translation: *Homage to Sextus Propertius* is arguably his finest work. Samuel Beckett went one step further: in order to find his own voice he first abandoned his native language altogether. He wrote in French, then translated himself triumphantly back into English, thereby transforming himself from a minor disciple of Joyce into one of the most original writers of the century.[1]

Modernism has long ago run its course, but then, as Mrs Thatcher discovered, so too has Little Englandism. The Common Market and

1 I have always believed that the Americans were at the sharp end of Modernism in poetry for two reasons. First, they had nothing to lose; the great tradition from Chaucer to Shakespeare to Milton to Pope to the Romantics was not really their concern, although they paid lip-service to it. Second, they wanted, above all, to 'make it new'; this meant creating a new poetic language for themselves – a language that expressed American vernacular rhythms, a language not bound by the Shakespearean iambic pentameter. It was a question not just of a different accent but of an altogether different voice. William Carlos Williams had a patriotic 'Little American' programme for this, the aesthetic equivalent of isolationism. But all the others, even the most sophisticated – like Eliot and Stevens, whom Williams loathed – were doing something similar in their different ways.

the prospect – come the millennium – of a Federal Europe have had sharp cultural repercussions. The present generation of readers is far less insular than their mothers and fathers and, for them, European poetry is no longer alien and beside the point. There are now three British publishing houses – Bloodaxe, Carcanet and Anvil – who specialize in contemporary European poetry in translation, and they seem to have shown that the project is sufficiently profitable even for Penguin to put a toe back in the water.

But the wider the net has been spread, the less influential the traditional continental sources of inspiration have become. Contemporary French poetry, in particular, seems to have very little audience outside France. The focus has shifted east towards the countries that, until recently, were behind the Iron Curtain. Even before the curtain rusted away, the literature of Eastern Europe had acquired a certain spurious chic and was being praised for the wrong reasons. Calvino put it best: in his novel *If on a Winter's Night a Traveller*, Arkadian Porphyrich, Director General of the State Police Archives of the country of Ircania, has this to say:

Nobody these days holds the written word in such high esteem as police states do ... What statistic allows one to identify the nations where literature enjoys true consideration better than the sums appropriated for controlling it and suppressing it? Where it is the object of such attentions, literature gains an extraordinary authority, inconceivable in countries where it is allowed to vegetate as an innocuous pastime, without risks.

For nearly two centuries, the literature of countries like Poland, Czechoslovakia and Hungary, which were squeezed between hostile major powers and accustomed to one form or another of foreign domination, has been the object of this dubious style of official attention. In those circumstances, it ceases to be a marginal, leisure-time activity and becomes crypto-politics. One hundred and fifty years ago, for example, the poet Sandor Petöfi was a key figure in Hungarian political life for two equally compelling reasons: because he played a leading role in the 1848 War of Independence and died in battle; and because, in a country where the official language of parliament and law was Latin and the Habsburg court spoke German, he was the first major poet to use the vernacular. According to Georg Lukács, Petöfi's poem 'John the Hero' was doubly important in its day: it was written in the native language and, for the first time in Hungarian literature, it was also a work in which the Magyar-speaking hero was a peasant with nationalistic ideals, not a nobleman. Together those two elements added up to a kind of revolutionary political act. For the Hungarian, Petőfi is revered both as a major poet and a national hero. The discussion group where the 1956 revolution was born was called the Petőfi Club. Similarly, in Poland there is a long and honoured tradition of what they call 'Aesopian language' – political discussion masquerading as works of the imagination. 'All political discussions happened in novels and poems. There were no politics, but there were writers.' That was said by Zdzislaw Najder, a literary academic, Conrad scholar and one-time political exile. Now the wheel of history has turned and Najder is an adviser to the president of the post-communist Polish government. Borges, who had experienced some of the same pressures, put it even more succinctly: 'Censorship is the mother of metaphor.'

So when the communist lid came down over Eastern Europe in 1948, the writers, after their brief democratic honeymoon between the two world wars, found themselves back in a situation they knew depressingly well. The stakes, however, had been raised out of all recognition. Even the most private poets with no political interests at all found themselves politicized willy-nilly, because to write about the private world without reference to the canons of socialist realism was, both by decree and by definition, a subversive activity. They became, that is, what poets in those countries had always been: an opposition in hiding, witnesses for the prosecution. But what was at stake now was not the old game of politics pretending to be poetry, the continuation of politics by other means. It was, instead, something far more important: the survival of ordinary human values – sanity, decency, self-respect – in an ocean of corruption and hypocrisy. Zbigniew Herbert's great poem 'The Envoy of Mr Cogito' was more than a refusal to go gently into that good night; it was also a refusal to accept the lies and compromises that made for the good life in communist Poland:

go upright among those who are on their knees
among those with their backs turned and those toppled in the dust

you were saved not in order to live
you have little time you must give testimony

> be courageous when the mind deceives you be courageous
> in the final account only this is important

Herbert's authority as a poet is also a moral authority, and that is
not a role writers in the West are accustomed to. Milton was
probably the last English poet with that degree of ethical prestige,
and when Shelley called poets 'unacknowledged legislators' he was
indulging in the sheerest wishful thinking.

That wishful thinking has lingered on. Right up until the moment
when Marxism imploded and the Iron Curtain collapsed, there were
writers in the West who seemed secretly to aspire to the importance
suppression confers on the suppressed, believing that the situation of
their colleagues further east was somehow, despite the restrictions
and deprivations of their daily lives, creatively glamorous. They
hankered after a society in which what they wrote was taken so
seriously that it might result in persecution, jail or exile. Better that,
they implied, than the frivolous Western democracies where any-
thing goes and nothing matters. Whence the spectacle of some of
England's most pampered writers standing up at international
literary conferences and claiming, straight-faced, that life in Mrs
Thatcher's Britain was as threatening as life under the KGB. It was a
line of argument that went down well with Writers' Union bosses
and their official 'socialist-artist' side-kicks, but to non-party writers
it sounded like the whining of spoiled children who resented being
left out of whatever spiritual tribulation was currently fashionable.

Even allowing for the self-serving elements in the argument – self-
dramatization, seriousness by association – it made a terrible
mockery of the reality in which communist-bloc poets had to work.
It is one thing to take account of the pressures they had to overcome,
to give due credit to their strength, shrewdness and wit, their refusal,
in the face of considerable temptation, to fake their responses
and do the official right thing. But to hanker after disaster in
order to authenticate or dignify your own efforts is something else
entirely.

By these same dim lights, the Eastern Europeans had a further
advantage: they were mostly of a generation that had experienced
first-hand the horrors of totalitarianism, first under the Nazis, then
under the Stalinists. For the radical chic, that meant they couldn't
help but be serious if the first creative battle they had to fight was

with Adorno's famous dictum: 'To write lyric poetry after Ausch-
witz is barbaric.'

As a muse, however, terror has a limited shelf-life. I can think of
very few writers who faced it head-on and came out with great art.
(Paul Celan, Primo Levi and the Polish short story writer, Tadeusz
Borowski, are the obvious exceptions.) Terror and horror are also
not the right words to describe how artists responded to forty-odd
years of leaden communist oppression, with its philistine apparat-
chiks, petty rule-makers and time-servers. The situation they had to
face was not like that of Nazi Germany or Stalinist Russia; it was
more like living in an England ruled by old-fashioned trade-union
barons and with the cultural standards set by the Bollinger bolshe-
viks. 'How would you like it,' a Polish writer once asked me, 'if you
had to submit every word you wrote to the literary editor of the
Daily Mirror?' In Miroslav Holub's words, 'the Czech experience
was the epitome of the age-old struggle of intellect with codified
stupidity.' The proper response was not horror; it was indignation,
contempt, muffled outrage.

The only decent alternative was silence, as Holub discovered as a
student, after the communist coup in Czechoslovakia in 1948:

The leader of the communist students announced that the [Students'] Union
had just been dissolved and a blind hysterical sort of *yurodivy* ['visionary']
young man began screaming about his vision of the May Day parade in
which we would all march and sing the Russian songs.

At that moment I realized that there is no poetry not only because of
Auschwitz, that there are no words, that there is no identity, that we are
completely isolated in the crowds of quasi-*yurodivy* colleagues, that there is
no 'civilian' poetry . . . and no programme except to shut up.

So we entered literature by shutting up. By complete silence. By a
complete distrust of everybody.

It was a perfect lesson in Creative Non-writing. It was a short-cut to an
almost biological feeling of the absurdity of everything, including one's
inner self . . .

Anything else that happened in literature could not even be named. It was
not modernism, nor post-modernism. It was plain self-defence; when you

are drowning, you may not care for theoretical, linguistic or literary denotations of your words or bubbles.[2]

The proper response to communist oppression, to its inertia and venality, to the sentimentality of 'socialist realism', was not dramatics or self-pity; it was sanity. Holub again:

Authenticity, living everyday authenticity, plain human speech, and the most ordinary human situation of these years were not only poetically viable but also the most telling argument.

The result was a poetry founded on a positively visceral reaction against the 'poetic'.

'I tend to find any old newspaper more absorbing than the finest edition of poems,' Tadeusz Różewicz said. 'Hence my sudden revulsion against Rilke. My motto was Norwid's "A proper word to name each thing." I was aiming at a poetry of absolute transparency, so that the dramatic material might be seen through the poem, just as in clear water you can see what is moving on the bottom. And so the form had to vanish, had to become transparent, it had to become identified with the subject of a given poem.'[3]

The minimalism Różewicz is talking about has less to do with aesthetics than with moral principles.

Zbigniew Herbert, who, in his pursuit of simplicity, has stripped his poetry even of punctuation without in any way disturbing its persistent lucidity, made a similar point in a poem called 'A Knocker':

There are those who grow
gardens in their heads
paths lead from their hair
to sunny and white cities

it's easy for them to write
they close their eyes
immediately schools of images
stream down from their foreheads

2 Miroslav Holub, 'Poetry against Absurdity', *Poetry Review*, Summer 1990, pp. 4–6.
3 'Tadeusz Różewicz in Conversation with Adam Czerniawski', *The New Review*, 25, 1976, p. 10. Quoted in Tadeusz Różewicz, *Conversation with the Prince*, London, 1982, p. 16.

my imagination
is a piece of board
my sole instrument
is a wooden stick

I strike the board
it answers me
yes – yes
no – no

It is typical of Herbert, who is a great ironist, that he should write about his strengths as though they were limitations beyond his control.

It is also typical of all the modern European poetry I most admire in writers as far apart as Finland and Greece. It is a poetry based on clarity, irony and a distaste for whatever is exaggerated or ornate or overstated, a poetry of private life, good behaviour and that much-abused term 'decency'. Perhaps it has something in common with the classicism advocated by Eliot and T. E. Hulme in the first great days of Modernism – classicism, that is, as a force for sanity, as opposed to the hothouse deformations of late Romanticism. If so, it is Modernism without the experimental hype. That does not mean that it is not often the result of intense experiment, but the experiments have one aim in common: the elimination of hype in the steady pursuit of emotional precision.

The poems in this anthology all appeared after World War II. I have chosen mostly from among established poets of a certain age for several reasons. First, this is a personal anthology, so I have concentrated on poets whose work I have lived with and admired for some time. Second, I want the book to demonstrate what is, in my view, the best in European poetry, not the most promising, because even the best is still very little known in Britain. Third, after the revolutions of 1989, the younger poets are inheriting a vastly changed scene where altogether different rules will apply. The last couple of years have seen the end not just of an empire but of a secular religion. Whatever happens now to European poetry, it is bound to be different from what has been produced in the last forty-five years. The demise of radical chic may take a little longer.

A. Alvarez
June 1991

PUBLISHERS NOTE

Translators are identified by their initials at the end of each poem;
where no translator is credited, the poem was written in English or
was translated into English by the author. A full list of translators
will be found at the end of the book.

POLAND

To Be a Mouse

To be a mouse. Preferably a field mouse. Or a garden mouse –
but not the kind that live in houses.
Man exudes an abdominable smell!
We all know it – birds, crabs, rats.
He provokes disgust and fear.
        Trembling.

To feed on wisteria blossoms, on the bark of palm trees,
to dig up roots in cold, humid soil
and to dance after a brisk night. To look at the full moon,
to reflect in one's eyes the sleek light of lunar
        agony.

To burrow in a mouse hole against the time when wicked Boreas
will search for me with his cold, bony fingers
so he can squeeze my little heart under the
                                    blade of his claw,

a cowardly mouse heart –
        a palpitating crystal.

Menton-Garavan, April 1956   [CM/LN]

Arithmetic

When you are alone
don't think you are alone.
He (she) is always with you.

Anywhere you go
you are followed.
The most faithful dog is not as faithful,
a shadow sometimes disappears,
he (she) – never.

That red-headed whore loafs in the entrance of a hotel
and with her is – not her double – she, another she.
That old man sneaks in after her like a cat
and with him, his inseparable companion.

Those two on a bed in contortions.
These two sit at the foot and wait, sadly bowing their heads.

Paris, June 1956   [CM/LN]

A Flamingo's Dream

Water water water. And nothing but water.
If only one inch of land! An inch of no-matter-what land!
To set foot on! Just an inch!

We begged the gods for that! All of them!
Water gods, land gods, southern gods, northern gods,
For an inch, a strip, a scrap of any kind of land!
No more than just enough to support the claw of one foot!
And nothing. Only water. Nothing except water.
Water water water.
If only a speck of land!
There is no salvation.

[CM/LN]

Imagerie d'Epinal
(On the death of Reik, Slansky and thousands of others)

The executioner yawned. The blood was still dripping from his axe.
'Don't cry, my child, don't, here's a lollipop.'

He took her in his arms. Stroked her. And she
                                        stared at the head.
At the sightless eyes. At the dumb lips.

It was her father's head. Later on, embalmed,
washed, it was stuck on a pole and prettily painted.

With that pole she marched in a parade on a sunny, populous road,
under her school placard:

                        'Happiness for all – to enemies death.'

1949   [CM/LN]

From Persian Parables

By great, swift waters
on a stony bank
a human skull lay shouting:
Allah la ilah.

And in that shout such horror
and such supplication
so great was its despair
that I asked the helmsman:

What is there left to cry for? Why is it still afraid?
What divine judgment could strike it again?

Suddenly a rising wave
took hold of the skull
and tossing it about
smashed it against the bank.

Nothing is ever over
– the helmsman's voice was hollow –
and there is no bottom to evil.

                [CM/LN]

From Notes Written in Obory

X was asked.
        if he believed in the objective existence of Parzota
– To believe in the objective existence of Parzota –
        that smacks of mysticism,
I am an old horse, you known, and a staunch
rationalist –

answered X.
The sequel was more interesting.

X persisted in his refusal to believe in the
                          objective existence of
       Parzota.
Who, the said Parzota, put him in a dungeon,
                        tortured him.
Yet everything would have been in perfect order
if not for one sad circumstance:
the stupid man of principle was so obstinate that
                        he died in the dungeon:
Poor Parzota! he will never know,
Sentenced as he was to eternal doubt
Whether he had objective existence.

[CM/LN]

Childhood of a Poet

Melos whispered words in his ear,
their meaning was incomprehensible.
Weaving them by twos, by threes
she would crown his forehead
with thorns.

She fed his heart with bitterness.
Till, overflowing with nausea, it exploded in a spasm
of joy
shared with nobody
nobody
nobody.

That was a sad childhood.
Sounds, remembrances, dreams
in which he always soared one inch above earth.
Then he fell.
The fall of a child . . .
The levitation of a poet.

[CM/LN]

Japanese Archery

I

The hand tells the bowstring:
    Obey me.

The bowstring answers the hand:
    Draw valiantly.

The bowstring tells the arrow:
    O arrow, fly.

The arrow answers the bowstring:
    Speed my flight.

The arrow tells the target:
    Be my light.

The target answers the arrow:
    Love me.

II

The target tells arrow, bowstring, hand and eye:
    Tat twam asi.

Which means in a sacred tongue:
    I am Thou.

III

(Footnote of a Christian:
    O Mother of God,

watch over the target, the bow, the arrow
    and the archer).

        [RL]

A Joke
To Gordon Craig

Bunches of carnations in a tin pitcher.
Beyond the window, is that a faun playing a flute?
In a fusty room the semi-darkness of dawn.
The lovers sleep. On the sill

the cat purrs. In its dream a rabble of birds.
She wakens like a bird and, trembling,
opens her eye on the alabaster
shaded mournfully by her streaming hair.

She found in it her wreath fished up from a river
and searches for his hand, looking for protection.
Then plunges into sleep again – into a flow, a flow . . .

Suddenly the door creaked softly. Somebody enters. Surprised.
Looks, hardly believes: My son – with a woman!
and retreats on tiptoe: O Hamlet! Hamlet!

Venice, September 1956   [CM/LN]

To a Roman, my Friend

Everything that lies in rubble
reaches tenderly at me:
the ruins of my Warsaw
the ruins of your Rome.

In April 'forty-six
I saw two old goats
searching for some special herbs
in the former Albrecht's Café
(now overgrown with nettles,
thistles, burdock, spear grass).
Their barefoot shepherdess
in graveyard stillness
stood gaping, a child, under a pathetic column that once adorned
          the fourth floor
                              of the Credit Society building,
where then it was just a fancy ornament
changed today into an orphaned pendicle
on a fragment of charred wall.

On the Aventino I met two goats, roamers of ruins,
and a barefoot shepherdess
staring at faded frescoes.

Thus after man's glory,
after his acts and disasters
goats arrive. Smelly,
comic and worthy goats
to search among remnants of glory
for medicinal herbs and forage
for earthly nourishment.

[CM/LN]

Taking a Walk

Temeh, Cain's wife, and Tirzah, Abel's widow,
were taking a walk along the edge of Eden, this side of the barbed-
    wire wall.
From the towers winged soldiers shouted warnings, gaily,
roguishly: Watch out! A million macrovolts! No doubt they
    exaggerated.
Thistles hardly breed here. Nearby, in the Mountains, dwarf pines.
Earth is like dry rot. A hundred days without rain. But
in one corner a colony of burdocks prospers,
also a settlement of toads. A little spring trickles there
from the underground waters of the river Pishon. In which river,
as is known from the Holy Writ (Genesis 2, 11), gold is
for the picking. And pure as gold. Young sons of Cain
toil on, extracting it, under guard, from dawn till night.
Not hard work. And profitable. And the air is brisk,
very healthful.
Rats would sneak to that spring from Eden,
also moles. For a change of climate? Of mood?

Temeh and Tirzah have so much to tell each other!
About that row.
And who started it? They were brothers, after all.
It's easy to say: a row. For one — an eternal spout of tears!
A mystery of widowhood. To the other — the subject of incessant
adoration for her husband, ox-necked labourer.
While Temeh jabbers about muscles (and saliva flicks from the
    corners of her mouth)

Tirzah thinks: . . . a jerk . . . but mine was tender-skinned.
A nimble-legged hunter. Swifter than any deer. And the string of his
    bow
sounded like the golden string of a lute. On which lute the mother
    Eve
thrums in the brown of dusk, in the twilight, when she yearns after
the snake, when he was young and handsome, after the lost, ha,
happiness; and the stupid old fool (he suspects nothing)
      asks her to thrum
            and thrum
– he finds in this thrumming his dream, the first, when the Master
    Surgeon
opened his side, took out a rib, anachronistic and painful,
and after coating it nicely in mellow flesh, split it somwhat at the
    bottom,
so that the complementary sex came into being – till he finds his
    dream again
and dozes, poor cuckold, falls asleep, snores . . .

Thus Temeh and Tirzah walk into the night. Till
Cain's call resounds, rumbling like thunder.
Temeh minces off at top speed, while Tirzah returns with a trailing
    gait
to a litter of autumn leaves. Here autumn is everlasting.

                [CM/LN]

To Leopold Labedz

. . . frisst der Grimm seine Gestaltungen in sich hinein.
                                 Hegel

What can I do if for you I am
lumen obscurum? Believe me, in myself
I contain my whole self as a bright point.
Even transparent. But
                     a misunderstanding,
semantic, today reigns over all and sundry.

Yet I do not forget, my Hippolyte:
we are both well-behaved boys

in straw hats and white middy blouses
with navy-blue trim, who early in the morning
went chasing butterflies. But who, at nightfall,
run after zigzags of lightning,
panting, exhausted. In vain . . .
                              For not even those zigzags
will tear through Chaos! Nothing will tear Chaos
apart. It tears itself apart. Eating into
itself, piece after piece, insa-
tiable.
        And there's nothing I can do about it,
dear friend.

Paris, July 1963   [CM/LN]

The Bride
For our fortieth anniversary

Let him not unveil her with his eye
Before he washes it in the light
Of morning, in the snows of a distant mountain,
In a gentle hill of herbs,
In the stream of the cantatas of Johann Sebastian
Bach.

Let him not put his hand on her
Before he cleanses it of violence. From blood.
Spilled. Assented to. Before he engraves it
With tenderness, good deeds,
With the toil of labouring in earth the mother,
With playing a harpsichord or ocarina.

Let him not bring his lips closer to her
Before he rinses off the lie,
Before he drinks from the source of live water.
Before he burns them pure in live fire
Before he sanctifies them in the Tabernaculum
Of grace and sweetness.

                    [CM/LN]

CZESLAW MILOSZ   1911–

Dedication

You whom I could not save
Listen to me.
Try to understand this simple speech as I would be ashamed of
    another.
I swear, there is in me no wizardry of words.
I speak to you with silence like a cloud or a tree.

What strengthened me, for you was lethal.
You mixed up farewell to an epoch with the beginning of a new one,
Inspiration of hatred with lyrical beauty,
Blind force with accomplished shape.

Here is the valley of shallow Polish rivers. And an immense bridge
Going into white fog. Here is a broken city,
And the wind throws the screams of gulls on your grave
When I am talking with you.

What is poetry which does not save
Nations or people?
A connivance with official lies,
A song of drunkards whose throats will be cut in a moment,
Readings for sophomore girls.
That I wanted good poetry without knowing it,
That I discovered, late, its salutary aim,
In this and only this I find salvation.

They used to pour millet on graves or poppy seeds
To feed the dead who would come disguised as birds.
I put this book here for you, who once lived
So that you should visit us no more.

Warsaw, 1945

Mid-twentieth-century Portrait

Hidden behind his smile of brotherly regard,
He despises the newspaper reader, the victim of the dialectic of
  power.
Says: 'Democracy,' with a wink.
Hates the physiological pleasures of mankind,
Full of memories of those who also ate, drank, copulated,
But in a moment had their throats cut.
Recommends dances and garden parties to defuse public anger.

Shouts: 'Culture!' and 'Art!' but means circus games really.

Utterly spent.
Mumbles in sleep or anaesthesia: 'God, oh God!'
Compares himself to a Roman in whom the Mithras cult has mixed
  with the cult of Jesus.
Still clings to old superstitions, sometimes believes himself to be
  possessed by demons.
Attacks the past, but fears that, having destroyed it,
He will have nothing on which to lay his head.
Likes most to play cards, or chess, the better to keep his own
  counsel.

Keeping one hand on Marx's writings, he reads the Bible in private.
His mocking eye on processions leaving burned-out churches.
His backdrop: a horseflesh-colored city in ruins.
In his hand: a memento of a boy 'fascist' killed in the Uprising.

Kraków, 1945

Preface

First, plain speech in the mother tongue.
Hearing it, you should be able to see
Apple trees, a river, the bend of a road,
As if in a flash of summer lightning.

And it should contain more than images.
It has been lured by singsong,

A daydream, melody. Defenseless,
It was bypassed by the sharp, dry world.

You often ask yourself why you feel shame
Whenever you look through a book of poetry.
As if the author, for reasons unclear to you,
Addressed the worse side of your nature,
Pushing aside thought, cheating thought.

Seasoned with jokes, clowning, satire,
Poetry still knows how to please.
Then its excellence is much admired.
But the grave combats where life is at stake
Are fought in prose. It was not always so.

And our regret has remained unconfessed.
Novels and essays serve but will not last.
One clear stanza can take more weight
Than a whole wagon of elaborate prose.

Gift

A day so happy.
Fog lifted early, I worked in the garden.
Hummingbirds were stopping over honeysuckle flowers.
There was no thing on earth I wanted to possess.
I knew no one worth my envying him.
Whatever evil I had suffered, I forgot.
To think that once I was the same man did not embarrass me.
In my body I felt no pain.
When straightening up, I saw the blue sea and sails.

Berkeley, 1971

Secretaries

I am no more than a secretary of the invisible thing
That is dictated to me and a few others.
Secretaries, mutually unknown, we walk the earth
Without much comprehension. Beginning a phrase in the middle

Or ending it with a comma. And how it all looks when completed
Is not up to us to inquire, we won't read it anyway.

Berkeley, 1975

After Paradise

Don't run anymore. Quiet. How softly it rains
On the roofs of the city. How perfect
All things are. Now, for the two of you
Waking up in a royal bed by a garret window.
For a man and a woman. For one plant divided
Into masculine and feminine which longed for each other.
Yes, this is my gift to you. Above ashes
On a bitter, bitter earth. Above the subterranean
Echo of clamorings and vows. So that now at dawn
You must be attentive: the tilt of a head,
A hand with a comb, two faces in a mirror
Are only forever once, even if unremembered,
So that you watch what is, though it fades away,
And are grateful every moment for your being.
Let that little park with greenish marble busts
In the pearl-gray light, under a summer drizzle,
Remain as it was when you opened the gate.
And the street of tall peeling porticoes
Which this love of yours suddenly transformed.

Winter

The pungent smells of a California winter,
Grayness and rosiness, an almost transparent full moon.
I add logs to the fire, I drink and I ponder.

'In Ilawa,' the news item said, 'at age 70
Died Aleksander Rymkiewicz, poet.'

He was the youngest in our group. I patronized him slightly,
Just as I patronized others for their inferior minds
Though they had many virtues I couldn't touch.

And so I am here, approaching the end
Of the century and of my life. Proud of my strength
Yet embarrassed by the clearness of the view.

Avant-gardes mixed with blood.
The ashes of inconceivable arts.
An omnium-gatherum of chaos.

I passed judgement on that. Though marked myself.
This hasn't been the age for the righteous and the decent.
I know what it means to beget monsters
And to recognize in them myself.

You, moon, You, Aleksander, fire of cedar logs.
Waters close over us, a name lasts but an instant.
Not important whether the generations hold us in memory.
Great was that chase with the hounds for the unattainable meaning
    of the world.

And now I am ready to keep running
When the sun rises beyond the borderlands of death.
I already see mountain ridges in the heavenly forest
Where, beyond every essence, a new essence waits.

You, music of my late years, I am called
By a sound and a color which are more and more perfect.

Do not die out, fire. Enter my dreams, love.
Be young forever, seasons of the earth.

Preparation

Still one more year of preparation.
Tomorrow at the latest I'll start working on a great book
In which my century will appear as it really was.
The sun will rise over the righteous and the wicked.
Springs and autumns will unerringly return,
In a wet thicket a thrush will build his nest lined with clay
And foxes will learn their foxy natures.

And that will be the subject, with addenda. Thus: armies
Running across frozen plains, shouting a curse
In a many-voiced chorus; the cannon of a tank
Growing immense at the corner of a street; the ride at dusk
Into a camp with watchtowers and barbed wire.

No, it won't happen tomorrow. In five or ten years.
I still think too much about the mothers
And ask what is man born of woman.
He curls himself up and protects his head
While he is kicked by heavy boots; on fire and running,
He burns with bright flame; a bulldozer sweeps him into a clay pit.
Her child. Embracing a teddy bear. Conceived in ecstasy.

I haven't learned yet to speak as I should, calmly.

A Portrait with a Cat

A little girl looks at a book with a picture of a cat
Who wears a fluffy collar and has a green velvet frock.
Her lips, very red, are half opened in a sweet reverie,
This takes place in 1910 or 1912, the painting bears no date.
It was painted by Marjorie C. Murphy, an American
Born in 1888, like my mother, more or less.
I contemplate the painting in Grinnell, Iowa,
At the end of the century. That cat with his collar
Where is he? And the girl? Am I going to meet her,
One of those mummies with rouge, tapping with their canes?
But this face: a tiny pug nose, round cheeks,
Moves me so, quite like a face that I, suddenly awake
In the middle of the night, saw by my side on a pillow.
The cat is not here, he is in the book, the book in the painting.
No girl, and yet she is here, before me
And has never been lost. Our true encounter
Is in the zones of childhood. Amazement called love,
A thought of touching, a cat in velvet.

Berkeley, 1985

And yet the Books

And yet the books will be there on the shelves, separate beings,
That appeared once, still wet
As shining chestnuts under a tree in autumn,
And, touched, coddled, began to live
In spite of fires on the horizon, castles blown up,
Tribes on the march, planets in motion.
'We are,' they said, even as their pages
Were being torn out, or a buzzing flame
Licked away their letters. So much more durable
Than we are, whose frail warmth
Cools down with memory, disperses, perishes.
I imagine the earth when I am no more:
Nothing happens, no loss, it's still a strange pageant,
Women's dresses, dewy lilacs, a song in the valley.
Yet the books will be there on the shelves, well born,
Derived from people, but also from radiance, heights.

Berkeley, 1986

TYMOTEUSZ KARPOWICZ   1921–

Lesson in Silence

Whenever a butterfly
folded its wings
too violently –
they cried: quiet please!

If but the wing
of a scared bird
brushed a sunray –
they cried: silence please!

Thus they taught
elephants to walk
noiselessly over a drum
man over earth

Trees rose
soundlessly in the field
as hair does
in terror

   [AC]

False Alarm

The cry
brought out neighbours
then the ambulance
and the police

But the street's stone flowed clear
no hands were bloodstained
no heart lead-packed

They dispersed
declared the alarm false –

As if only blood and lead
revealed to men
man's agony

    [AC]

Dream

What terrible dream
caused the poet
to jump out of his sleep
like a stag from a burning forest?

– The butterfly in his metaphor
had veiled him with its wings

and the door-knob he had described
twitched

    [AC]

Ecclesiastes

there is a time for opening the eyes and closing the bed
time for donning a shirt and shedding sleep
time for drowsy soap and half-awakened skin
time for the hair-brush and for sparks in the hair
time for trouser-legs time for shoe-laces time for buttons
for laddered stockings for the slipper's blindness
time for the fork and for the knife time for sausages and boiled eggs
time for the tram time for the conductress time for the policeman
time for good morning and time for goodbye
time for carrots peas and parsley
for tomato soup and shepherd's pie
time for trussing chicken and releasing forbidden speeds of thought
time for a cinema ticket or a ticket to nowhere
to a river perhaps perhaps to a cloud
there is finally a time for closed eyelids and the open bed
time for past present and future
praesens historicum and plusquamperfectum

time perfect and imperfect
time from wall to wall

     [AC]

The Pencil's Dream

When the pencil undresses for sleep
he firmly decides
to sleep stiffly
and blackly

he is helped in it
by the inborn inflexibility
of all the piths of the world
the spinal pith of the pencil
will break but cannot be bent

he will never dream of
waves or hair
only of a soldier standing at attention
or coffins

what finds its place in him
is straight
what is beyond is crooked
good night

     [CM]

TADEUSZ RÓŻEWICZ   1921–

The Survivor

I am twenty-four
led to slaughter
I survived.

The following are empty synonyms:
man and beast
love and hate
friend and foe
darkness and light.

The way of killing men and beasts is the same
I've seen it:
truckfuls of chopped-up men
who will not be saved.

Ideas are mere words:
virtue and crime
truth and lies
beauty and ugliness
courage and cowardice.

Virtue and crime weigh the same
I've seen it:
in a man who was both
criminal and virtuous.

I seek a teacher and a master
may he restore my sight hearing and speech
may he again name objects and ideas
may he separate darkness from light.

I am twenty-four
led to slaughter
I survived.

    [AC]

Living Star

What days entwine me
soft and perfumed
like beards of Assyrian merchants
so many days so many days
finely clustered

what nights swallow me
as dark as the gullet
wrapped in a red mucous membrane
so many nights so many nights
in the belly of a whale

My friend came
a hole in his forehead
and tore away fine beards
he tore apart the belly of delight
he ripped out
the limp spine of a reptile
and injected a new white marrow
like a star of quicksilver.

[AC]

A Visit

I couldn't recognize her
when I came in here
just as well it's possible
to take so long arranging these flowers
in this clumsy vase

'Don't look at me like that'
she said
I stroke the cropped hair
with my rough hand
'they cut my hair' she says
'look what they've done to me'

now again that sky-blue spring
begins to pulsate beneath the transparent
skin of her neck as always
when she swallows tears

why does she stare like that
I think well I must go
I say a little too loudly

and I leave her,
a lump in my throat

[AC]

Chestnut

Saddest of all is leaving
home on an autumn morning
when there is no hope of an early return

The chestnut father planted in front
of the house grows in our eyes

mother is tiny
you could carry her in your arms

On the shelf
jars full of preserves
like sweet-lipped goddesses
have retained the flavour
of eternal youth

soldiers at the back of the drawer
will stay leaden till the end of the world

while God almighty who mixed in
bitterness with the sweetness
hangs on the wall helpless
and badly painted

childhood is like the worn face
on a golden coin that rings
true.

1947–48   [AC]

Abattoirs

Pink quartered ideals
hang in abattoirs

Shops are selling
clowns'
motley death-masks
stripped off the faces
of us who live
who have survived
staring
into the eye-socket of war.

[AC]

'But whoever sees'

But whoever sees my mother
in a purple smock in a white hospital
trembling
stiffening
with a wooden smile
and white gums

who for fifty years had faith
but now weeps and says
'I don't know . . . I don't know'

her face is like a large smudged tear
she clasps her hands like a frightened
little girl
her lips are blue

but whoever sees my mother
a hounded little animal
with a bulging eye

he

oh I would like to bear her upon my heart
and nourish her with sweetness

1947–48   [AC]

What Luck

What luck I can pick
berries in the wood
I thought
there is no wood no berries.

What luck I can lie
in the shade of a tree
I thought trees
no longer give shade.

What luck I am with you
my heart beats so
I thought man
has no heart.

    [AC]

Pigtail

When all the women in the transport
had their heads shaved
four workmen with brooms made of birch twigs
swept up
and gathered up the hair

Behind clean glass
the stiff hair lies
of those suffocated in gas chambers

there are pins and side combs
in this hair

The hair is not shot through with light
is not parted by the breeze
is not touched by any hand
or rain or lips

In huge chests
clouds of dry hair
of those suffocated
and a faded plait
a pigtail with a ribbon
pulled at school
by naughty boys.

The Museum, Auschwitz, 1948   [AC]

Massacre of the Boys

The children cried 'Mummy!
But I have been good!
It's dark in here! Dark!'

See them They are going to the bottom
See the small feet
they went to the bottom Do you see
that print
of a small foot here and there

pockets bulging
with string and stones
and little horses made of wire

A great closed plain
like a figure of geometry
and a tree of black smoke
a vertical
dead tree
with no star in its crown.

The Museum, Auschwitz, 1948   [AC]

The Colour of her Eyes and Questions

Has my love
deep-blue eyes
with no silver speck
No

Does my dear
have hazel eyes
with a golden spark
No

Does my love
have black eyes
without light
No

My dear has eyes
which fall on me
like grey
autumnal rain

1954   [AC]

Who's Absent
To the memory of Zbyszek my little pupil

Who is drowned
who isn't here

Who is screaming so terribly
who is silent

Who is without lips

What is this
surfacing
how horrifyingly this small body
grows

all this commotion all these words
who isn't here
it's he

that good boy
has turned
into a thing
which stealthily
comes out of the water
and tears the mother apart

1955   [AC]

Leave Us

Forget us
forget our generation
live like humans
forget us

we envied
plants and stones
we envied dogs

I'd rather be a rat
I told her then

I'd rather not be
I'd rather sleep
and wake when war is over
she said her eyes shut

Forget us
don't enquire about our youth
leave us

1955–57   [AC]

Posthumous Rehabilitation

The dead have remembered
our indifference
The dead have remembered
our silence

The dead have remembered
our words

The dead see our snouts
laughing from ear to ear
The dead see
our bodies rubbing against each other
The dead hear
clucking tongues

The dead read our books
listen to our speeches
delivered so long ago

The dead scrutinize our lectures
join in previously terminated
discussions
The dead see our hands
poised for applause

The dead see stadiums
ensembles and choirs declaiming rhythmically

all the living are guilty

little children
who offered bouquets of flowers
are guilty
lovers are guilty
guilty are poets

guilty are those who ran away
and those that stayed
those who were saying yes
those who said no
and those who said nothing

the dead are taking stock of the living
the dead will not rehabilitate us

1957   [AC]

A Meeting

I meet the dead more and more often
they are strangely animated
their mouths are open they talk a lot
some of them foam
like soap

recently I came across a largish group of the dead
who sat in rows on chairs
their cheeks rosy
they laughed clapped sat down
were indignant got up
made personal remarks

among old corpses
bustled the young
they don't know
they're scatter-brained
they move their arms and legs
drive cars embrace new
standpoints and wives who are still warm

there was one experienced deceased
who kept winking at me
roguishly
and even tried
to be reborn
in the eyes of the assembly

November 1956 (at the Writers' Congress in Warsaw) [AC]

To the Heart

I watched
an expert cook
he would thrust his hand
into the windpipe
pushing it through

into the sheep's
inside
and there in the quick
would grasp the heart
his fingers closing
round the heart
would rip out the heart
with one pull
yes
he certainly was an expert

1959   [AC]

They Shed the Load

He comes to you
and says

you are not responsible
either for the world or the end of the world
the load has been lifted off your shoulders
you are like children and birds
go, play

and they play

they forget
that contemporary poetry
means struggle for breath

1959   [AC]

Leda

Leda with strong
arms
and thighs

Leda pressed
against the bird's
supple body

her head thrown back
a mysterious smile
absent
she receded

I was torn away
from her
pushed aside

blood
flowed
from
my lips and tongue

1965   [AC]

Draft for a Contemporary Love Poem

For surely whiteness
is best described through greyness
bird through stone
sunflowers
in December

in the past love poems
described flesh
described this and that
eyelashes for instance

surely redness
should be described
through greyness sun through rain
poppies in November
lips at night

the most telling
description of bread
is one of hunger
it includes
the damp porous centre
the warm interior

sunflowers at night
breasts belly thighs of Cybele

a spring-like
transparent description
of water
is the description of thirst
of ashes
desert
it conjures up a mirage
clouds and trees enter
the mirror

Hunger deprivation
absence
of flesh
is the description of love
the contemporary love poem

Summer 1963   [AC]

Proofs

Death will not correct
a single line of verse
she is no proof-reader
she is no sympathetic
lady editor

a bad metaphor is immortal

a shoddy poet who has died
is a shoddy dead poet

a bore bores after death
a fool keeps up his foolish chatter
from beyond the grave

                    [AC]

In the Theatre of Shades

From the crack
between me and the world
between me and the object
from the distance
between noun and pronoun
poetry
struggles to emerge

it has to make
for itself such tools
shape such forms
as would hook on to me
and the word
like two shores
which diverge
continually

torn apart
it tries once again to
bring together
compare
unite
it struggles
to the surface

I go away

1963   [AC]

'I was sitting in an easy-chair'

I was sitting in an easy-chair
I stopped reading
suddenly I heard
my heart beating
it was so unexpected
as though a stranger had entered into me
and hammered with a clenched fist

some unknown creature
locked inside me
there was something indecent
in its battering with no relation
to me
to my abstract thought

1979   [AC]

ZBIGNIEW HERBERT   1924–

Two Drops

No time to grieve for roses, when the forests are burning.
                                        Słowacki

The forests were on fire –
they however
wreathed their necks with their hands
like bouquets of roses

People ran to the shelters –
he said his wife had hair
in whose depths one could hide

Covered by one blanket
they whispered shameless words
the litany of those who love

When it got very bad
they leapt into each other's eyes
and shut them firmly

So firmly they did not feel the flames
when they came up to the eyelashes

To the end they were brave
To the end they were faithful
To the end they were similar
like two drops
stuck at the edge of a face

                    [PS]

Arion

This is he – Arion –
the Grecian Caruso
concertmaster of the ancient world
expensive as a necklace

or rather as a constellation
singing
to the ocean billows and traders in silks
to the tyrants and mule herders
The crowns blacken on the tyrants' heads
and the sellers of onion cakes
for the first time err in their figures to their own disadvantage

What Arion is singing about
nobody here could say exactly
the essential thing is that he restores world harmony
the sea gently rocks the land
fire talks to water without hatred
in the shadow of one hexameter lie down
wolves and roedeer goshawks and doves
and the child goes to sleep on the lion's mane
as in a cradle
Look how the animals are smiling
People are living on white flowers
and everything is just as good
as it was in the beginning

This is he – Arion
expensive and multiple
cause of giddiness
standing in a blizzard of images
he has eight fingers like an octave
and he sings

Until from the blue in the west
unravel the luminous threads of saffron
which show that night is coming close
Arion with a friendly shake of his head
says good-bye to
the mule herders and tyrants
the shopkeepers and philosophers
and in the harbour mounts the back
of a tame dolphin

– I'll be seeing you –

How handsome Arion is
— say all the girls —
when he floats out to sea
alone
with a garland of horizons on his head

[PS]

A Knocker

There are those who grow
gardens in their heads
paths lead from their hair
to sunny and white cities

it's easy for them to write
they close their eyes
immediately schools of images
stream down from their foreheads

my imagination
is a piece of board
my sole instrument
is a wooden stick

I strike the board
it answers me
yes — yes
no — no

for others the green bell of a tree
the blue bell of water
I have a knocker
from unprotected gardens

I thump on the board
and it prompts me
with the moralist's dry poem
yes — yes
no — no

[CM]

Maturity

It's good what happened
it's good what's going to happen
even what's happening right now
it's o.k.

> In a nest pleated from the flesh
> there lived a bird
> its wings beat about the heart
> we mostly called it: unrest
> and sometimes: love

> evenings
> we went along the rushing sorrow river
> in the river one could see oneself
> from head to toe

> now
> the bird has fallen to the bottom of the clouds
> the river has sunk into the sand

> helpless as children
> and practised as old men
> we are – simply – free
> that is – ready to depart

> In the night a nice old man arrives
> and coaxes us with an enticing gesture
> – who are you? – we ask in alarm

> – Seneca – say those who finished grammar school
> and those who don't know Latin
> just call me: the deceased

[PS]

The Rain

When my older brother
came back from war
he had on his forehead a little silver star

and under the star
an abyss

a splinter of shrapnel
hit him at Verdun
or perhaps at Grünwald
(he'd forgotten the details)

he used to talk much
in many languages
but he liked most of all
the language of history

until losing breath
he commanded his dead pals to run
Roland Kowalski Hannibal

he shouted
that this was the last crusade
that Carthage soon would fall
and then sobbing confessed
that Napoleon did not like him

we looked at him
getting paler and paler
abandoned by his senses
he turned slowly into a monument

into musical shells of ears
entered a stone forest

and the skin of his face
was secured
with blind dry
buttons of eyes

nothing was left him
but touch

what stories
he told with his hands
in the right he had romances
in the left soldier's memories

they took my brother
and carried him out of town
he returns every fall
slim and very quiet
he does not want to come in
he knocks at the window for me

we walk together in the streets
and he recites to me
improbable tales
touching my face
with blind fingers of rain

[CM]

Rosy Ear

I thought
but I know her so well
we have been living together so many years

I know
her bird-like head
white arms
and belly

until one time
on a winter evening
she sat down beside me
and in the lamplight
falling from behind us
I saw a rosy ear

a comic petal of skin
a conch with living blood
inside it

I didn't say anything then –

it would be good to write
a poem about a rosy ear
but not so that people would say

what a subject he chose
he's trying to be eccentric

so that nobody even would smile
so that they would understand that I proclaim
a mystery

I didn't say anything then
but that night when we were in bed together
delicately I essayed
the exotic taste
of a rosy ear

    [CM]

Silk of a Soul

Never
did I speak with her
either about love
or about death

only blind taste
and mute touch
used to run between us
when absorbed in ourselves
we lay close

I must
peek inside her
to see what she wears
at her centre

when she slept
with her lips open
I peeked

and what
and what
do you think
I caught sight of

I was expecting
branches
I was expecting
a bird
I was expecting
a house
by a lake great and silent

but there
on a glass counter
I caught sight of a pair
of silk stockings

my God
I'll buy her those stockings
I'll buy them

but what will appear then
on the glass counter
of the little soul

will it be something
which cannot be touched
even with one finger of a dream

[PS]

Parable of the Russian Emigrés

It was in the year twenty
or perhaps twenty-one
the Russian émigrés
came to us

tall blond people
with visionary eyes
and women like a dream

when they crossed the market-place
we used to say — migratory birds

they used to attend the *soirées* of the gentry
everyone would whisper – look what pearls

but when the lights of the ball were extinguished
helpless people remained

the grey newspapers were continuously silent
only solitaire showed pity

the guitars beyond the windows would cease playing
and even dark eyes faded

in the evening a samovar with a whistle
would carry them back to their family railway-stations

after a couple of years
only three of them were spoken about
the one who went mad
the one who hanged himself
she to whom men used to come

the rest lived out of the way
slowly turning into dust

>   This parable is told by Nicholas
>   who understands historical necessities
>   in order to terrify me i.e. to convince me

[PS]

Episode in a Library

A blonde girl is bent over a poem. With a pencil sharp as a lancet she transfers the words to a blank page and changes them into strokes, accents, caesuras. The lament of a fallen poet now looks like a salamander eaten away by ants.

When we carried him away under machine-gun fire, I believed that his still warm body would be resurrected in the word. Now as I watch the death of the words, I know there is no limit to decay. All that will be left after us in the black earth will be scattered syllables. Accents over nothingness and dust.

[PS]

The Wind and the Rose

Once in a garden there grew a rose. A wind fell in love with her. They were completely different, he – light and fair; she – immobile and heavy as blood.

There came a man in wooden clogs and with his thick hands he plucked the rose. The wind leapt after him, but the man slammed the door in his face.

– O that I might turn to stone – wept the unlucky one – I was able to go round the whole world, I was able to stay away for years at a time, but I knew that she was always there waiting.

The wind understood that, in order really to suffer, one has to be faithful.

[PS]

Hen

The hen is the best example of what living constantly with humans leads to. She has completely lost the lightness and grace of a bird. Her tail sticks up over her protruding rump like a too large hat in bad taste. Her rare moments of ecstasy, when she stands on one leg and glues up her round eyes with filmy eyelids, are stunningly disgusting. And in addition, that parody of song, throat-slashed supplications over a thing unutterably comic: a round, white, maculated egg.

The hen brings to mind certain poets.

[CM]

Apollo and Marsyas

The real duel of Apollo
with Marsyas
(absolute pitch
versus immense range)
takes place in the evening
when as we already know
the judges

have awarded victory to the god

bound tight to a tree
meticulously stripped of his skin
Marsyas
howls
before the howl reaches his tall ears
he reposes in the shadow of that howl

shaken by a shudder of disgust
Apollo is cleaning his instrument

only seemingly
is the voice of Marsyas
monotonous
and composed of single vowel
Aaa

in reality
Marsyas relates
the inexhaustible wealth
of his body

bald mountains of liver
white ravines of aliment
rustling forests of lung
sweet hillocks of muscle
joints bile blood and shudders
the wintry wind of bone
over the salt of memory
shaken by a shudder of disgust
Apollo is cleaning his instrument

now to the chorus
is joined the backbone of Marsyas
in principle the same A
only deeper with the addition of rust

this is already beyond the endurance
of the god with nerves of artificial fibre

along a gravel path
hedged with box

the victor departs
wondering
whether out of Marsyas' howling
there will not some day arise
a new kind
of art – let us say – concrete

suddenly
at his feet
falls a petrified nightingale

he looks back
and sees
that the hair of the tree to which Marsyas was fastened
is white
completely

    [CM]

Our Fear

Our fear
does not wear a night shirt
does not have owl's eyes
does not lift a coffin lid
does not extinguish a candle

does not have a dead man's face either

our fear
is a scrap of paper
found in a pocket
'warn Wójcik
the place on Długa Street is hot'

our fear
does not rise on the wings of the tempest
does not sit on a church tower
it is down-to-earth

it has the shape
of a bundle made in haste

with warm clothing
provisions
and arms

our fear
does not have the face of a dead man
the dead are gentle to us
we carry them on our shoulders
sleep under the same blanket

close their eyes
adjust their lips
pick a dry spot
and bury them

not too deep
not too shallow

[CM]

From Mythology

First there was a god of night and tempest, a black idol without eyes, before whom they leaped, naked and smeared with blood. Later on, in the times of the republic, there were many gods with wives, children, creaking beds, and harmlessly exploding thunderbolts. At the end only superstitious neurotics carried in their pockets little statues of salt, representing the god of irony. There was no greater god at that time.

Then came the barbarians. They too valued highly the little god of irony. They would crush it under their heels and add it to their dishes.

[CM]

The Return of the Proconsul

I've decided to return to the emperor's court
once more I shall see if it's possible to live there
I could stay here in this remote province

under the full sweet leaves of the sycamore
and the gentle rule of sickly nepotists

when I return I don't intend to commend myself
I shall applaud in measured portions
smile in ounces frown discreetly
for that they will not give me a golden chain
this iron one will suffice

I've decided to return tomorrow or the day after
I cannot live among vineyards nothing here is mine
trees have no roots houses no foundations the rain is glassy flowers
    smell of wax
a dry cloud rattles against the empty sky
so I shall return tomorrow or the day after in any case I shall return

I must come to terms with my face again
with my lower lip so it knows how to curb its scorn
with my eyes so they remain ideally empty
and with that miserable chin the hare of my face
which trembles when the chief of guards walks in

of one thing I am sure I will not drink wine with him
when he brings his goblet nearer I will lower my eyes
and pretend I'm picking bits of food from between my teeth
besides the emperor likes courage of convictions
to a certain extent to a certain reasonable extent
he is after all a man like everyone else

and already tired by all those tricks with poison
he cannot drink his fill incessant chess
this left cup is for Drusus from the right one pretend to sip
then drink only water never lose sight of Tacitus
go out into the garden and come back when they've taken away the
    corpse

I've decided to return to the emperor's court
yes I hope that things will work out somehow

[CM]

Elegy of Fortinbras
for C.M.

Now that we're alone we can talk prince man to man
though you lie on the stairs and see no more than a dead ant
nothing but black sun with broken rays
I could never think of your hands without smiling
and now that they lie on the stone like fallen nests
they are as defenceless as before The end is exactly this
The hands lie apart The sword lies apart The head apart
and the knight's feet in soft slippers

You will have a soldier's funeral without having been a soldier
the only ritual I am acquainted with a little
There will be no candles no singing only cannon-fuses and bursts
crepe dragged on the pavement helmets boots artillery horses drums
    drums I know nothing exquisite
those will be my manoeuvres before I start to rule
one has to take the city by the neck and shake it a bit

Anyhow you had to perish Hamlet you were not for life
you believed in crystal notions not in human clay
always twitching as if asleep you hunted chimeras
wolfishly you crunched the air only to vomit
you knew no human thing you did not know even how to breathe

Now you have peace Hamlet you accomplished what you had to
and you have peace The rest is not silence but belongs to me
you chose the easier part an elegant thrust
but what is heroic death compared with eternal watching
with a cold apple in one's hand on a narrow chair
with a view of the ant-hill and the clock's dial

Adieu prince I have tasks a sewer project
and a decree on prostitutes and beggars
I must also elaborate a better system of prisons
since as you justly said Denmark is a prison
I go to my affairs This night is born
a star named Hamlet We shall never meet
what I shall leave will not be worth a tragedy

It is not for us to greet each other or bid farewell we live on
   archipelagos
and that water these words what can they do what can they do
   prince

   [CM]

Pebble

The pebble
is a perfect creature

equal to itself
mindful of its limits

filled exactly
with a pebbly meaning

with a scent which does not remind one of anything
does not frighten anything away does not arouse desire

its ardour and coldness
are just and full of dignity

I feel a heavy remorse
when I hold it in my hand
and its noble body
is permeated by false warmth

      – Pebbles cannot be tamed
      to the end they will look at us
      with a calm and very clear eye

         [CM]

Revelation

Two perhaps three
times
I was sure
I would touch the essence
and would know

the web of my formula
made of allusions as in the Phaedo
had also the rigour
of Heisenberg's equation

I was sitting immobile
with watery eyes
I felt my backbone
fill with quiet certitude

earth stood still
heaven stood still
my immobility
was nearly perfect

    the postman rang
    I had to pour out the dirty water
    prepare tea

    Siva lifted his finger
    the furniture of heaven and earth
    started to spin again

    I returned to my room
    where is that perfect peace
    the idea of a glass
    was being spilled all over the table

    I sat down immobile
    with watery eyes
    filled with emptiness
    i.e. with desire

If it happens to me once more
I shall be moved neither by the postman's bell
nor by the shouting of angels

I shall sit
immobile
my eyes fixed
upon the heart of things

a dead star

a black drop of infinity

[CM]

Tongue

Inadvertently I passed the border of her teeth and swallowed her agile tongue. It lives inside me now, like a Japanese fish. It brushes against my heart and my diaphragm as if against the walls of an aquarium. It stirs silt from the bottom.

She whom I deprived of a voice stares at me with big eyes and waits for a word.

Yet I do not know which tongue to use when speaking to her – the stolen one or the one which melts in my mouth from an excess of heavy goodness.

[CM]

Why the Classics

I

in the fourth book of the Peloponnesian War
Thucydides tells among other things
the story of his unsuccessful expedition

among long speeches of chiefs
battles sieges plague
dense net of intrigues of diplomatic endeavours
the episode is like a pin
in a forest

the Greek colony Amphipolis
fell into the hands of Brasidas
because Thucydides was late with relief

for this he paid his native city
with lifelong exile

exiles of all times
know what price that is

II

generals of the most recent wars
if a similar affair happens to them
whine on their knees before posterity
praise their heroism and innocence

they accuse their subordinates
envious colleagues
unfavourable winds

Thucydides says only
that he had seven ships
it was winter
and he sailed quickly

III

if art for its subject
will have a broken jar
a small broken soul
with a great self-pity

what will remain after us
will be like lovers' weeping
in a small dirty hotel
when wall-paper dawns

[CM]

What Mr Cogito Thinks about Hell

The lowest circle of hell. Contrary to prevailing opinion it is inhabited neither by despots nor matricides, nor even by those who go after the bodies of others. It is the refuge of artists, full of mirrors, musical instruments, and pictures. At first glance this is the most luxurious infernal department, without tar, fire, or physical tortures.

Throughout the year competitions, festivals, and concerts are held here. There is no climax in the season. The climax is permanent and almost absolute. Every few months new trends come into being and nothing, it appears, is capable of stopping the triumphant march of the avant-garde.

Beelzebub loves art. He boasts that already his choruses, his poets, and his painters are nearly superior to those of heaven. He who has better art has better government – that's clear. Soon they will be able to measure their strength against one another at the Festival of the Two Worlds. And then we will see what remains of Dante, Fra Angelico, and Bach.

Beelzebub supports the arts. He provides his artists with calm, good board, and absolute isolation from hellish life.

[JC/BC]

Mr Cogito Thinks of Returning to the City where He Was Born

If I went back there
probably I wouldn't find
even a shadow from my house
or the trees of childhood
or the cross with an iron plate
the bench where I whispered incantations
chestnuts and blood
or a single thing that is ours

all that was saved
is a flagstone
with a circle drawn in chalk
I stand in the centre
on one leg
the moments before jumping

I cannot grow up
although years go by
and planets and wars
roar above

I stand in the centre
motionless as a statue
on a single leg
before the leap to finality

the circle of chalk turns red
like old blood
while all around
piles of ash are growing
up to my shoulders
up to my mouth

    [JC/BC]

The Envoy of Mr Cogito

Go where those others went to the dark boundary
for the golden fleece of nothingness your last prize

go upright among those who are on their knees
among those with their backs turned and those toppled in the dust

you were saved not in order to live
you have little time you must give testimony

be courageous when the mind deceives you be courageous
in the final account only this is important

and let your helpless Anger be like the sea
whenever you hear the voice of the insulted and beaten

let your sister Scorn not leave you
for the informers executioners cowards – they will win
they will go to your funeral and with relief will throw a lump of
    earth
the woodborer will write your smoothed-over biography

and do not forgive truly it is not in your power
to forgive in the name of those betrayed at dawn

beware however of unnecessary pride
keep looking at your clown's face in the mirror
repeat: I was called – weren't there better ones than I

beware of dryness of heart love the morning spring
the bird with an unknown name the winter oak

light on a wall the splendour of the sky
they don't need your warm breath
they are there to say: no one will console you

be vigilant – when the light on the mountains gives the sign – arise
    and go
as long as blood turns in the breast your dark star

repeat old incantations of humanity fables and legends
because this is how you will attain the good you will not attain
repeat great words repeat them stubbornly
like those crossing the desert who perished in the sand

and they will reward you with what they have at hand
with the whip of laughter with murder on a garbage heap

go because only in this way will you be admitted to the company of
    cold skulls
to the company of your ancestors: Gilgamesh Hector Roland
the defenders of the kingdom without limit and the city of ashes

Be faithful Go

    [JC/BC]

ADAM ZAGAJEWSKI   1945—

Late Beethoven
I haven't yet known a man who loved virtue as strongly as one loves beauty.
                                                                    Confucius

Nobody knows who she was, the Immortal
Beloved. Apart from that, everything is
clear. Feathery notes rest
peacefully on the threads of the staff
like martins just come
from the Atlantic. What would I have to be
in order to speak about him, he who's still
growing. Now we are walking alone
without ghosts or banners. Long live
chaos, say our solitary mouths.
We know that he dressed carelessly,
that he was given to fits of avarice, that he wasn't
always fair to his friends.
Friends are a hundred years
late with their impeccable smiles. Who
was the Immortal Beloved? Certainly,
he loved virtue more than beauty.
But a nameless god of beauty dwelled
in him and compelled his obedience.
He improvised for hours. A few minutes
of each improvisation were noted down.
These minutes belong neither to the nineteenth
nor to the twentieth century; as if hydrochloric
acid burned a window in velvet, thus
opening a passage to even
smother velvet, thin as
a spiderweb. Now they name
ships and perfumes after him. They don't know who
the Immortal Beloved was, otherwise
new cities and pâtés would bear her
name. But it's useless. Only velvet
growing under velvet, like a leaf hidden

safely in another leaf. Light in darkness.
Unending adagios. That's how tired freedom
breathes. Biographers argue only
over details. Why he tormented
his nephew Karl so much. Why
he walked so fast. Why he didn't go
to London. Apart from that, everything is clear.
We don't know what music is. Who speaks
in it. To whom it is addressed. Why it is
so obstinately silent. Why it circles and returns
instead of giving a straight answer
as the Gospel demands. Prophecies
were not fulfilled. The Chinese didn't reach
the Rhine. Once more, it turned out that
the real world doesn't exist, to the immense
relief of antiquaries. The secret was hidden
somewhere else, not in soldiers'
knapsacks, but in a few notebooks.
Grillparzer, he, Chopin. Generals are
cast in lead and in tinsel to
give hell's flame a moment of respite
after kilowatts of straw. Unending adagios,
but first and foremost joy, wild
joy of shape, the laughing sister of death.

                                        [RG]

A River

Poems from poems, songs
from songs, paintings from paintings,
always this friendly
impregnation. On the other bank
of the river, within range of being,
soldiers are marching. A black army,
a red army, a green army,
the iron rainbow. In between, smooth
water, an indifferent wave.

                    [RG]

Good Friday in the Tunnels of the Métro

Jews of various religions mcct
in the tunnels of the Métro, rosary beads
spilled from someone's tender fingers.

Above them priests sleep after their Lenten supper,
above them the pyramids of synagogues and churches
stand like the rocks a glacier left behind.

I listened to the *St Matthew's Passion*,
which transforms pain into beauty.
I read the *Death Fugue* by Celan
transforming pain into beauty.

In the tunnels of the Métro no transformation of pain,
it is there, it persists and is keen.

[RG]

In the Encyclopedias, No Room for Osip Mandelstam

In the encyclopedias once again no room for
Osip Mandelstam again he is
homeless still it's so difficult to find a flat
How to register in Moscow it's nearly impossible
The Caucasus still calls him Asia's lowland forest
roars these days haven't arrived yet
Someone else picks up pebbles on the Black Sea beaches
This shifting investigation goes on though the uniform
is of new cut and its wooden-headed tailor
almost fell over bowing
You close a book it sounds like a gunshot
White dust from the paper tickles your nose a Latin
evening is here it snows nobody will come tonight
it's bedtime but if he knocks at your thin door
let him in

[RG]

CZECHOSLOVAKIA

VLADIMÍR HOLAN   1905–80

Human Voice

Stone and star do not force their music on us,
flowers are silent, things hold something back,
because of us, animals deny
their own harmony of innocence and stealth,
the wind has always its chastity of simple gesture
and what song is only the mute birds know,
to whom you tossed an unthreshed sheaf on Christmas Eve.

To be is enough for them and that is beyond words. But we,
we are afraid not only in the dark,
even in the abundant light
we do not see our neighbour
and desperate for exorcism
cry out in terror: 'Are you there? Speak!'

                          [JM/IM]

Daybreak

It is the hour when the priest goes to mass
up the devil's back.
It is the hour when the heavy bag of dawn
is zipped up the human spine.
It is the hour of frost and no sun
yet the stone is warm
because it moves.
It is the hour when the lake freezes round its shores
and man in his heart.
It is the hour when dreams are nothing more
than fleas nipping the skin of Marsyas.
It is the hour when trees ripped by the deer
bind their wounds with resin.
It is the hour when elves pick up
the splintered words of time.

It is the hour when merely for love
one dares descend the stalagmite cave of tears
which held back in secret worked their hidden will.
It is the hour when you have to write a poem
and say it differently, quite differently.

[JM/IM]

Meeting in a Lift

We stepped into the lift. The two of us, alone.
We looked at each other and that was all.
Two lives, a moment, fullness, bliss.
At the fifth floor she got out and I went on up
knowing I would never see her again,
that it was a meeting once and for all,
that if I followed her I would be like a dead man in her tracks
and that if she came back to me
it would only be from the other world.

[JM/IM]

Deep in the Night

'How not to be!' you ask yourself and in the end say it aloud . . .
But tree and stone are silent
though each is born of the word and therefore dumb
since the word is afraid of what it has become.
But *names* they still have. Names: pine,
maple, aspen . . . And names: feldspar,
basalt, phonolite, love. Beautiful names,
afraid only of what they have become.

[JM/IM]

Snow

It began to snow at midnight. And certainly
the kitchen is the best place to sit,

even the kitchen of the sleepless.
It's warm there, you cook yourself something, drink wine
and look out of the window at your friend eternity.
Why care whether birth and death are merely points
when life is not a straight line.
Why torment yourself eyeing the calendar
and wondering what is at stake.
Why confess you don't have the money
to buy Saskia shoes?
And why brag
that you suffer more than others.

If there were no silence here
the snow would have dreamed it up.
You are alone.
Spare the gestures. Nothing for show.

[JM/IM]

Verses

It is the time when the cabbage is served with wrath
and the calf with hate,
it is the time when death draws wine from nightshade,
it is the time when the blinder you are the more you stare,
it is the time when field boundaries are ploughed up,
it is the time when the hot tear knows
that it cries alone,
it is the time when the wolf grabs letter and book,
it is the time when the searchlight is on the spirit,
it is the time when you *cannot* love your own unhappiness
because it is everyone's.

[JM/IM]

Reminiscence II
To František Tichý

After hours of searching everywhere in vain
for pimpernel, we came out of the wood

and halted at high noon in the heather.
The air was baked like a sheet of tin. We looked
at the slope on the other side, thickly grown
with bushes and trees. They were rigid, like us.
I was about to ask something
when in the unmoving mass
of frozen enchantment a single tree
in a single spot
suddenly began to tremble
like a quarter-tone, yet soundless.
You would have said it was from careless joy,
the spirit of adventure.
But the tree began to rustle
like the rustle of silver turning black.
Then it began to quiver
like the skirt of a woman who touches
a man's clothes while reading a book in an asylum.
And then the tree began to shake and sway
as if shaken and swayed by someone
staring into the dark-eyed depths of love –
and I felt I was meant to die that moment . . .

'Don't be afraid,' my father said, 'it's an aspen.'
But I still remember how he paled
when we came there later on
and saw beneath the tree an empty chair.

[JM/IM]

Ubi nullus ordo, sed perpetuus horror

To live is terrible since you have to stay
with the appalling reality of these years.
Only the suicide thinks he can leave by the door
that is merely painted on the wall.
There is not the slightest sign that the Comforter will come.

In me the heart of poetry bleeds.

[JM/IM]

After St Martin's Day II

It was some time after Martinmas.
I was walking across the Gahatagat
plateau. I was in the sort of mood
when I didn't know which day it was.
But the snow had been falling and falling. It covered everything.
And at one moment the wind blew so sharply
I lowered my head
and suddenly saw with shrinking heart
always a step ahead of me
a fresh footprint

There wasn't a living soul around.
Who was it there in front of me?

It was I walking in front of myself.

[JM/IM]

Fourth Month

April mist. One ray of sun
pale as a blind man's stick inches its way,
though more certain than a week ago.
Cold hands, warm heart.

You too have more than a feeling . . . But that is all.
If danger threatens, you have no defence.
If happiness, you are powerless.

[JM/IM]

Glimpsed

Glimpsed from the train, which takes shadow for truth.
But she was truly beautiful
and bareheaded,

bareheaded as if an angel
had left his head there
and gone off with the hat.

[JM/IM]

Dream

The dry depths at the borders of memory
fray out into hairs that reach to hell.
Continence is shamelessly insistent. Laughter.
I have never taken men seriously,
says Lady Macbeth
and she inspects her hand
bloody from the murder of drunken mosquitoes.

[JM/IM]

During an Illness

A melting icicle, a leaking tap,
counting drops of medicine.

Tibet sees by water. We by tears.

[JM/IM]

Twelfth Night

The day of candles which lick
the carp bones of Christmas Eve.
But the wooden mortar for grinding poppy-seed
is very beautiful
in the deep foreground of the straw wall,
and beautiful this antique stillness,
and a week gone hasn't deceived time's seeming.
It's freezing and yet the tombstone is warm.
Because it moves.

[JM/IM]

Goodbye

Once more the storm is rising from fate's black quarter.
The mind feels faint,
bemused like a body turned inside out.
Who is that dancing in the bats'-wing cloak?
Who was struck dumb by the rattle of what he saw?
The water in the well lures youth, a man seeks the spring.
All that is over. There are words
one must not speak of.
You will never keep the promise you made.
The skull has dreamed your eyes.

[JM/IM]

For Himself

So many apples and no apple-tree! But
now there are no more apples here.
So much passion and no love! But
now there are no unchristened here.
Every man for himself
and we have time only for moments.
It won't last.

[JM/IM]

ANTONÍN BARTUŠEK   1921—

The Twentieth Century

We took snapshots as we went.
The click of the shutter tended to wake us
from sleep. Children
wore their smiles quite differently
from the ancient custom on this meadow
while the mothers, unsuspecting and abstracted,
occupied themselves with a distant truth.
It was hot. Strawberries ripened by the wayside.
All at once summer was not named after our longing . . .
The absent sea dozed off into a deep-blue sky-like sleep.
But since there was in fact no sky
we asked each and every signpost the way,
only to learn
where the lake ends in a blue silence . . .
I could also tell you of the woods . . . they too
exposed their credible faces to our lenses . . .
We took snapshots as we went, you see.
The truth came out in negative.

[GT]

Reality

The wailing of a child between two and three at night.
The night full of darkness, like a cathedral gargoyle,
like a tombstone swallowed by its own shadow . . .
like the faces I used to know,
like the faces that used to know me.
Somewhere the forest is assuming its own shape.
The wailing of a child between two and three at night.
Both my watch and my eyes are slow.

One afternoon it all ended.
One afternoon it all began.
Reality.

[GT]

Poetry

Tell me, what has last night in common
with today's morning on this shore
whose sand is soaked with the translucent water of sleep,
dragging me down to the bottom.
The fishes of words float lazily past me,
seeking a surface to leap from
and breathe the air,
pretending for a brief moment
that they are able to fly.
It is dark under the surface of the skin.
The ages are rusting there.
Above, the gentle silvery scales of light –
half beautiful maiden, half silent fish.

[GT]

Exile from Paradise

Fenced in by duration, the day
did not seem to exist. But a distant
breath of autumn
secretly imposed itself
on gardens and parks.
Timelessness continued. Eve turned away
while Adam beside her on a bench
was dozing. It was noon, a fallen angel
was turning into a serpent,
heavenly manna was dropping on the souls
of lovers, sweetly sustaining them. The leaves
shuddered at their impending fall.
The apple of sin was ripening.

But Adam slept
and therefore could not sin.
As he awoke from sleep
the angel of destruction kissed his forehead.
He sensed that he loved Eve
who had sinned.
The breath of autumn passed
through the park, the leaves shuddered
at their impending fall. Nursemaids
and young mothers were pushing prams,
the children howled, in dingy flats
the air was stifling, irritable men
went out to the pub and dreamed of adultery.
Heavenly manna sweetly dropped
on lovers' lips in dark and secret corners.
Our childhood this afternoon
was still intact:
at nightfall we kissed reality,
no longer a virgin.
The lights went on in the windows,
Eve, bending over her work-box,
was sewing clothes for her child.
Adam, a little drowsy,
was looking for a chance to slip away.
Exile from paradise continued.

[EO]

Simonetta Vespucci

Breasts beaten by thunder
like cymbals.
It's only a short step, sir,
to my room.
You may, if you wish,
copulate with me.
Gently run your hand
over my shimmering skin,
the envy of alabaster.

Small veins showing blue
on opened thighs,
as in quartz.
Empty the sky
around my halo.
Bone laid to bone
by the gravedigger
as he digs a fresh grave.
The proud profile in the landscape
with the river Lethe,
with the river and an unknown
Italian lake.

The scream of your throat
reaches the belly's cavern.
The flame's spearpoint
has cut right through your middle.
The dress, slipped off the shoulder,
no longer conceals anything.

And again May
with bleary eyes
is exploring your loins.
There's nothing ruin can't do.
All that's left is a gold
serpent necklace,
time biting its own tail.

Man looks about,
his eyes wandering,
as if looking for
someone he knows.

[EO]

Snapshot from a Family Outing

The anchors are dropped.
Sun-tanned Ulysses
has stepped on the beach
where graceful strange girls

with hips like the moon
over the cemetery wall
are washing their linen,
leaning against their menfolk.

Wearily the sailors
have raised to their lips
moss-grown cups with the empty
echo of the seabed.

The ship, momentarily
forgotten
in the viewfinder,
sails on to the Lotus-Island.

[EO]

The Return of the Poets

Like silkworms
we meet our poets
for years cocooned
in misfortune.

For years shone the sun of darkness
blood fell instead of rain,
the mire of mud came
up to our mouths.

Then
in the green mulberries of hope
the quick eye could have discerned
ever so slight a movement in the branches.

In the leafy mulberry groves
in the cocoons of love
they spun their words into silken threads
of silent speech.

So we should not be naked
when once more we emerge
into the light
of reality.

[EO]

Epitaph

This is the city
where men are buried alive.
At first we tried
to pretend that
we had long been dead.
They declared us insane
and forced us
to drink with all the rest
the blood of all the rest.
It was sweet and horrible.
One day
we felt gorged with ourselves
with men being continually
buried alive.
We refused
to gorge ourselves on the warm blood.
So they made us
dig our grave
and shot us dead
through the back of our heads.
Now we were really dead,
now we hoped it really was the end.
But they revived us
so they could bury us alive.

[EO]

MIROSLAV HOLUB   1923—

In the Microscope

Here too are dreaming landscapes,
lunar, derelict.
Here too are the masses,
tillers of the soil.
And cells, fighters
who lay down their lives
for a song.

Here too are cemeteries,
fame and snow.
And I hear murmuring,
the revolt of immense estates.

[IM]

Pathology

Here in the Lord's bosom rest
the tongues of beggars,
the lungs of generals,
the eyes of informers,
the skins of martyrs,

in the absolute
of the microscope's lenses.

I leaf through Old Testament slices of liver,
in the white monuments of brain I read
the hieroglyphs
of decay.

Behold, Christians,
Heaven, Hell, and Paradise
in bottles.
And no wailing,
not even a sigh.

Only the dust moans.
Dumb is history
strained
through capillaries.

Equality dumb. Fraternity dumb.

And out of the tricolours of mortal suffering
we day after day
pull
threads of wisdom.

                [GT]

Death in the Evening

High, high.

Her last words wandered across the ceiling
like clouds.
The sideboard wept.
The apron shivered
as if covering an abyss.

The end. The young ones had gone to bed.

But towards midnight
the dead woman got up,
put out the candles (a pity to waste them),
quickly mended the last stocking,
found her fifty nickels
in the cinnamon tin
and put them on the table,
found the scissors fallen behind the cupboard,
found a glove
they had lost a year ago,
tried all the door knobs,
tightened the tap,
finished her coffee,
and fell back again.

In the morning they took her away.
She was cremated.
The ashes were coarse
as coal.

[GT]

Five Minutes after the Air Raid

In Pilsen,
twenty-six Station Road,
she climbed to the third floor
up stairs which were all that was left
of the whole house,
she opened her door
full on to the sky,
stood gaping over the edge.

For this was the place
the world ended.

Then
she locked up carefully
lest someone steal
Sirius
or Aldebaran
from her kitchen,
went back downstairs
and settled herself
to wait
for the house to rise again
and for her husband to rise from the ashes
and for her children's hands and feet to be stuck back in place.

In the morning they found her
still as stone,
sparrows pecking her hands.

[GT]

Alphabet

Ten million years
from the Miocene
to the primary school in Ječná Street.

We know everything
from *a* to *z*.

But sometimes the finger stops
in that empty space between *a* and *b*,
empty as the prairie at night,

between *g* and *h*,
deep as the eyes of the sea,

between *m* and *n*,
long as man's birth,

sometimes it stops
in the galactic cold
after the letter *z*,
at the beginning and the end,

trembling a little
like some strange bird.

Not from despair.

Just like that.

    [EO]

The Fly

She sat on a willow-trunk
watching
part of the battle of Crécy,
the shouts,
the gasps,
the groans,
the trampling and the tumbling.

During the fourteenth charge
of the French cavalry
she mated
with a brown-eyed male fly
from Vadincourt.

She rubbed her legs together
as she sat on a disembowelled horse
meditating
on the immortality of flies.

With relief she alighted
on the blue tongue
of the Duke of Clervaux.

When silence settled
and only the whisper of decay
softly circled the bodies

and only
a few arms and legs
still twitched jerkily under the trees,

she began to lay her eggs
on the single eye
of Johann Uhr,
the Royal Armourer.

And thus it was
that she was eaten by a swift
fleeing
from the fires of Estrées.

[GT]

Polonius

Behind every arras
he does his duty
unswervingly.
Walls are his ears,
keyholes his eyes.

He slinks up the stairs,
oozes from the ceiling,
floats through the door
ready to give evidence,
prove what is proven,
stab with a needle
or pin on an order.

His poems always rhyme,
his brush is dipped in honey,
his music flutes
from marzipan and cane.

You buy him
by weight, boneless,
a pound of wax flesh,
a pound of mousy philosophy,
a pound of jellied
flunkey.

And when he's sold out
and the left-overs wrapped
in a tasselled obituary,
a paranoid funeral notice,

and when the spore-creating mould
of memory
covers him over,
when he falls
arse-first to the stars,

the whole continent will be lighter,
earth's axis straighten up
and in night's thunderous arena
a bird will chirp in gratitude.

[IM]

Love

Two thousand cigarettes.
A hundred miles
from wall to wall.
An eternity and a half of vigils
blanker than snow.

Tons of words
old as the tracks
of a platypus in the sand.

A hundred books we didn't write.
A hundred pyramids we didn't build.

Sweepings.
Dust.

Bitter
as the beginning of the world.

Believe me when I say
it was beautiful.

[IM]

Wings

We have
microscopic anatomy
of the whale
this
is
reassuring
    William Carlos Williams

We have
a map of the universe
for microbes,
we have
a map of a microbe
for the universe.

We have
a Grand Master of chess
made of electronic circuits.

But above all
we have
the ability
to sort peas,
to cup water in our hands,
to seek
the right screw
under the sofa
for hours.

This
gives us
wings.

1953 [GT]

A Helping Hand

We gave a helping hand to grass –
      and it turned into corn.
We gave a helping hand to fire –
      and it turned into a rocket.
Hesitatingly,
cautiously,
we give a helping hand
to people,
to some people . . .

      [GT]

Žito the Magician

To amuse His Royal Majesty he will change water into wine.
Frogs into footmen. Beetles into bailiffs. And make a Minister

out of a rat. He bows, and daisies grow from his finger-tips.
And a talking bird sits on his shoulder.

There.

Think up something else, demands His Royal Majesty.
Think up a black star. So he thinks up a black star.
Think up dry water. So he thinks up dry water.
Think up a river bound with straw-bands. So he does.

There.

Then along comes a student and asks: Think up sine alpha
greater than one.

And Žito grows pale and sad: Terribly sorry. Sine is
between plus one and minus one. Nothing you can do about that.
And he leaves the great royal empire, quietly weaves his way
through the throng of courtiers, to his home
                                        in a nutshell.

                                              [GT]

A Boy's Head

In it there is a space-ship
and a project
for doing away with piano lessons.

And there is
Noah's ark,
which shall be first.

And there is
an entirely new bird,
an entirely new hare,
an entirely new bumble-bee.

There is a river
that flows upwards.

There is a multiplication table.

There is anti-matter.

And it just cannot be trimmed.

I believe
that only what cannot be trimmed
is a head.

There is much promise
in the circumstance
that so many people have heads.

[IM]

Suffering

Ugly creatures, ugly grunting creatures,
Completely concealed under the point of the needle,
    behind the curve of the Research Task Graph,
Disgusting creatures with foam at the mouth,
    with bristles on their bottoms,
One after the other
They close their pink mouths
They open their pink mouths
They grow pale
Flutter their legs
    as if they were running a very
    long distance,

They close ugly blue eyes,
They open ugly blue eyes
    and
    they're
    dead.

But I ask no questions,
no one asks any questions.

And after their death we let the ugly creatures
    run in pieces along the white expanse
    of the paper electrophore

We let them graze in the greenish-blue pool
    of the chromatogram
And in pieces we drive them for a dip
    in alcohol
    and xylol
And the immense eye of the ugly animal god
    watches their every move
    through the tube of the microscope
And the bits of animals are satisfied
like flowers in a flower-pot
    like kittens at the bottom of a pond
    like cells before conception.
But I ask no questions,
    no one asks any questions,

Naturally no one asks
Whether these creatures wouldn't have preferred
    to live all in one piece,
    their disgusting life
    in bogs
    and canals,
Whether they wouldn't have preferred to eat
    one another alive,
Whether they wouldn't have preferred to make love
    in between horror and hunger,
Whether they wouldn't have preferred to use
    all their eyes and pores to perceive
    their muddy stinking little world
Incredibly terrified,
Incredibly happy
In the way of matter which can do no more.

But I ask no questions,
    no one asks any questions,
Because it's all quite useless,
Experiments succeed and experiments fail,
Like everything else in this world,
    in which the truth advances
    like some splendid silver bulldozer
    in the tumbling darkness,

Like everything else in this world,
    in which I met a lonely girl
    inside a shop selling bridal veils,
In which I met a general covered
    with oak leaves,
In which I met ambulance men who could find no
    wounded,
In which I met a man who had lost
    his name,
In which I met a glorious and famous, bronze,
    incredibly terrified rat,
In which I met people who wanted to lay down
    their lives and people who wanted to lay down
    their heads in sorrow,
In which, come to think of it, I keep meeting my
    own self at every step.

          [GT]

Reality

The small worms of pain still wriggled
    in the limpid air,
The trembling died away and
Something in us bowed low before
    the fact of the operating-table
    the fact of the window
    the fact of space
    the fact of steel
    with seven blades.

The silence was inviolable
    like the surface of a mirror.

Though we wanted to ask
Where the blood was flowing
And
Whether you were still dead,
    darling.

     [IM]

The Prague of Jan Palach

And here stomp Picasso's bulls.
And here march Dali's elephants on spidery legs.
And here beat Schönberg's drums.
And here rides Señor de la Mancha.
And here the Karamazovs are carrying Hamlet.
And here is the nucleus of the atom.
And here is the cosmodrome of the Moon.
And here stands a statue without the torch.
And here runs a torch without the statue.
And it's all so simple. Where
Man ends, the flame begins –
And in the ensuing silence can be heard the crumbling
of ash worms. For
those milliards of people, taken by and large,
are keeping their traps shut.

[GT]

The Dead

After his third operation, his heart
riddled like an old fairground target,
he woke up on his bed
and said: Now I'll be fine,
fit as a fiddle. And have you ever seen
horses coupling?

He died that night.

And another dragged on through eight insipid years
like a river weed in an acid stream,
as if pushing up his pallid
skewered face over the cemetery wall.

Until that face eventually vanished.

Both here and there the angel of death
quite simply stamped his hobnailed boot
on their medulla oblongata.

I know they died the same way.
But I don't believe that they are
dead the same way.

      [EO]

Half a Hedgehog

The rear half had been run over,
leaving the head and thorax
and the front legs of the hedgehog shape.

A scream from a cramped-open
jaw. The scream of the mute is
more horrible than the silence after a flood,
when even black swans float
belly upwards.

And even if some hedgehog doctor were
to be found in a hollow trunk or under the leaves
in a beechwood there'd be no hope
for that mere half on Road E12.

In the name of logic,
in the name of the theory of pain,
in the name of the hedgehog god the father, the son
and the holy ghost amen,
in the name of games and unripe raspberries,
in the name of tumbling streams of love
ever different and ever bloody,
in the name of the roots which overgrow
the heads of aborted foetuses,
in the name of satanic beauty,
in the name of skin bearing human likeness,
in the name of all halves
and double helices, of purines
and pyrimidines

we tried to run over
the hedgehog's head with the front wheel.

And it was like guiding a lunar module
from a planetary distance,
from a control centre seized
by cataleptic sleep.

And the mission failed. I got out
and found a heavy piece of brick.
Half the hedgehog continued screaming. And now
the scream turned into speech,

prepared by
the vaults of our tombs:
Then death will come and it will have your eyes.

[EO]

HUNGARY

SÁNDOR WEÖRES   1913–89

The Colonnade of Teeth

I
The Colonnade of Teeth, where you have entered,
red marble hall: your mouth,
white marble columns: your teeth,
and the scarlet carpet you step on: your tongue.

II
You can look out of any window of time
and catch sight of still another face of God.
Lean out of the time of sedge and warblers:
God caresses.
Lean out of the time of Moses and Elias:
God haggles.
Lean out of the time of the Cross:
God's face is all blood, like Veronica's napkin.
Lean out of your own time:
God is old, bent over a book.

III
Head downwards, like Peter on his cross,
man hangs in the blue sky with flaring hair
and the earth trundles over the soles of his feet.
The one who sees
has sleepless eyes he cannot take from man.

IV
No sugar left for the child:
he stuffs himself with hen-droppings and finds what's sweet.
Every clod: lightless star!
Every worm: wingless cherub!

V
If you make hell, plunge to the bottom:
heaven's in sight there. Everything circles round.

VI

Man lays down easy roads.
The wild beast stamps a forest track.
And look at the tree: depth and height raying from it to every
    compass-point;
Itself a road, to everywhere!

VII

Once you emerge from the glitter of the last two columns
the cupola your hair skims is then infinity,
and a swirl of rose-leaves throws you down,
and all that lies below, your bridal bed: the whole world –
Here you can declare:
'My God, I don't believe in you!'
And the storm of rose-leaves will smile:
'But I believe in you: are you satisfied?'

[EM]

Orpheus Killed

I lie in a cold shaded courtyard, I am dead.
I am sobbing over my body, so many women, men.
Grief rolls from the drum and I start dancing. Who
killed me, why?
        I drift round the market, in palaces,
in taverns, among the flute-players, till in drink
I can say to the drunk: Look at me, I am
your hearts: engaged to death for the sake
of beggars and the blind.
        Stone I am and metal I am
on a slave's cross. The corpse is staring wide-eyed,
grief rolls from the drum and I dance. I am everything
and I am nothing: oh, look at me. I am everyone
and I am no one: stone and metal, many shapes,
on a slave's cross. Why did the priests kill me?
Did I slight their temple?

Dismembered I lie in the wasteland,
what urn is there for my white dust? Why
did the women tear me? Do they want my dead love?

Wolves of the famished earth prowl all round me,
decay rains rolling down and I start dancing.
Cain I am and saint I am: kneel at my feet.
Leper I am and clean I am: touch me. Body
moves, weak joints crack, cold tears trickle, he
sweats, sweats. Mindless I am and wise I am,
ask no questions, understand in silence. Dead I am
and alive I am, a dumb face, I. A wax-face
sacrifice turns skyward, ringed by staring horror, grief
rolls from the drum and I dance.
        No asking back
the body stretched on the cross. I lie harvested in the wasteland,
no asking back the grain laid up in barns.
Death's drum rolls, I whirl in the dance for ever,
the song flooding the valley refreshed by my blood,
my secret endless life entangled in the groves of death.

[EM]

Terra Sigillata

Epigrams of an ancient poet

Useless interrogation: I know nothing. An old man fallen asleep,
I wake as a baby, and you can read your learning from my
wide blue eyes; I only glimpse it in recidivist streams.

*

A red-fingered child pats grey cakes at the seaside,
I ask for one, he says no, not even for a real cake, no.
Well now, old prophets, what do you want from me? the twenty-
    four
sky prisms, when I look blind into hearts and read them.

*

If you want your fortune, I'll reel off your identity, your
    expectations,
but I'm deaf to my own words — no plundering secrets.

    *

'You say you're God's offspring: why do you scrape along like
    paupers?'
'Even Zeus himself, when he takes human steps on earth,
begs bread and water, parched, starved as a tramp.'

    *

The Dazzling is always coming to earth to beg for mud,
while his palace in heaven, stiff with gold, sighs for his return.

    *

The bowed-down carrier looks up: there he stands at the centre of
    the earth!
it is above his head that the sky's vault goes highest.

    *

Beautiful the lonely pine, beautiful the bee-wreathed rose,
beautiful the white funeral, most beautiful through all — their union.

    *

The treasures of a tree! Leaves, flowers, fruits.
How freely it gives them, clinging to the elements alone.

    *

The forest has modesty, the wolf hides his death in the shadows,
but a bought mourner will shrill without shame at a stranger's
    burial.

    *

The swindler doesn't slip up with his bogus balance-sheets when his
    heart is firm,
but when bursting out crying and taking pity on the innocent.

    *

Crime has majesty, virtue is holy; but what is the troubled heart
    worth?
There, crime is raving drunk and virtue is a jailer.

    *

The moment I slice the cocoon of my fate: my skull is the sky-dome,
fate-shuttling stars scuttle across its arch.

[EM]

In Memoriam Gyula Juhász*

Let the beasts whine at your grave my father
whine at your grave
let the beasts whine
between the byre and the blade
between the slaughterhouse and dunghill
between the clank of the chain and desolation
my mother as Hamlet said
let the old hunchbacked women whine
between the hospital and the glad rags
between the asylum and the lily-of-the-valley
between the cemetery and the frippery
and the wretches with buried ulcers
between stately doctors and strapping priests
all those paralysed by deferred release
on the far side of hope on the near side of confrontation

Let butterflies twist above the stream
Ophelia who drowned before we were born
the roseless thorn is yours
the profitless pain
the lacklustre ghost in a mourning frame
the falling on knees face in the mud
the humiliation boundless and endless
the dead body without a cross
the unredeemed sacrifice
the hopelessness that is for ever hopelessness

Let rabid dogs howl at your grave
let hollow phantoms hoot
my starry brother my bearded bride
the good is only a moment's presentiment
evil is not eternal malice
in the meantime blood flows
lacerated life cannot die
death is deathless liberty

* Hungarian poet, 1883–1937   [EM]

The Secret Country

One day we'll jump on a floating log, E Daj the distant is waiting for
   us,
we'll float on the log, wing-locked butterflies,
dance gently downwards through the traveller's-joy
beneath the sea, no one aware of us.

Below earth and sea there is a black lake,
motionless and mirror-sharp,
no one knows its chasms:
E Daj the distant is waiting for us,
one day we'll jump on a floating log, plunge in.

The old men say:
As long as we live,
everything we see
hangs in that mirror in the lake,
our faces, our figures
figured facing down.
The palms, the lianas, the foxes, the stars
all hang there in the mirror of the lake.

Short-lived the butterfly, but it visits the old farmhouse,
puttering about it with its whispering
wings, we hear them whispering,
we run, run into the house.
We don't speak to it, we don't speak to shadows.

It knocks at the door, knocks and knocks, breaks off, goes back
  home,
E Daj the distant is waiting for us.

The old men say:
Our faces and figures are reflected in the black lake,
no one sees its depths:
whatever is, was once in them,
whatever was once in them, falls back there,
and this is the eternal return.

The man throws his spear, bends his bow,
the woman scrapes a hole for the fire,
all look for handholds, build huts:
and this is how we live, hanging head down in the mirror of the lake,
one day we'll jump on a floating log, plunge in.
We can't see what lies below. E Daj the distant is waiting for us.

[EM]

Monkeyland

Oh for far-off monkeyland,
ripe monkeybread on baobabs,
and the wind strums out monkeytunes
from monkeywindow monkeybars.

Monkeyheroes rise and fight
in monkeyfield and monkeysquare,
and monkeysanatoriums
have monkeypatients crying there.

Monkeygirl monkeytaught
masters monkeyalphabet,
evil monkey pounds his thrawn
feet in monkeyprison yet.

Monkeymill is nearly made,
miles of monkeymayonnaise,
winningly unwinnable
winning monkeymind wins praise.

Monkeyking on monkeypole
harangues the crowd in monkeytongue,
monkeyheaven comes to some,
monkeyhell for those undone.

Macaque, gorilla, chimpanzee,
baboon, orangutan, each beast
reads his monkeynewssheet at
the end of each twilight repast.

With monkeysupper memories
the monkeyouthouse rumbles, hums,
monkeyswaddies start to march,
right turn, left turn, shoulder arms –

monkeymilitary fright
reflected in each monkeyface,
with monkeygun in monkeyfist
the monkeys' world the world we face.

[EM]

JÁNOS PILINSZKY   1921–81

Harbach 1944
To Gábor Thurzó

At all times I see them.
The moon brilliant. A black shaft looms up.
Beneath it, harnessed men
haul a huge cart.

Dragging that giant wagon
which grows bigger as the night grows
their bodies are divided among
the dust, their hunger and their trembling.

They are carrying the road, they are carrying the land,
the bleak potato fields,
and all they know is the weight of everything,
the burden of the skylines

and the falling bodies of their companions
which almost grow into their own
as they lurch, living layers,
treading each other's footsteps.

The villages stay clear of them,
the gateways withdraw.
The distance, that has come to meet them,
reels away back.

Staggering, they wade knee deep
in the low, darkly-muffled clatter
of their wooden clogs
as through invisible leaf litter.

Already their bodies belong to silence.
And they thrust their faces towards the height
as if they strained for a scent
of the far-off celestial troughs

because, prepared for their coming
like an opened stock-yard,
its gates flung savagely back,
death gapes to its hinges.

[JC/TH]

The French Prisoner

If only I could forget that Frenchman.
I saw him, a little before dawn, creeping past our hut
into the dense growth of the back garden
so that he almost merged into the ground.
As I watched he looked back, he peered all round –
at last he had found a safe hideout.
Now his plunder can be all his!
Whatever happens, he'll go no further.

And already he is eating, biting into the turnip
which he must have smuggled out under his rags.
He was gulping raw cattle-turnip!
Yet he had hardly swallowed one mouthful
before it vomited back up.
Then the sweet pulp in his mouth mingled
with joy and revulsion the same
as the happy and unhappy are coupled
in their bodies' ravenous ecstasy.

Only to forget that body, those convulsed shoulder blades,
the hands shrunk to bone,
the bare palm that crammed at his mouth, and clung there
so that it ate, too.
And the shame, desperate, furious,
of the organs savaging each other,
forced to tear from each other
their last shreds of kinship.

The way his clumsy feet had been left out
of the gibbering, bestial elation –
and splayed there, squashed beneath

the torture and rapture of his body.
And his glance – if only I could forget that!
Though he was choking, he kept on
forcing more down his gullet – no matter what –
only to eat – anything – this – that – even himself!

Why go on? Guards came for him.
He had escaped from the nearby prison camp.
And just as I did then, in that garden,
I am strolling here, among garden shadows, at home.
I look into my notes and quote:
'If only I could forget that Frenchman . . .'
And from my ears, from my eyes, my mouth
the scorching memory roars at me:

'I am hungry!' And suddenly I feel
the everlasting hunger
that poor creature has long since forgotten
and which no earthly nourishment can lessen.
He lives on me. And more and more hungrily!
And I am less and less sufficient for him.
And now he, who would have eaten anything,
is yelling for my heart.

> [JC/TH]

On the Wall of a KZ-Lager

Where you have fallen, you stay.
In the whole universe, this is your place.
Just this single spot.
But you have made this yours utterly.

The countryside evades you.
House, mill, poplar,
each thing strives to be free of you
as if it were mutating in nothingness.

But now it is you who stay.
Did we blind you? You continue to watch us.

Did we rob you? You enriched yourself.
Speechless, speechless, you testify against us.

[JC/TH]

Passion of Ravensbrück

He steps out from the others.
He stands in the square silence.
The prison garb, the convict's skull
blink like a projection.

He is horribly alone.
His pores are visible.
Everything about him is so gigantic.
everything is so tiny.

And this is all.
            The rest –
the rest was simply
that he forgot to cry out
before he collapsed.

[JC/TH]

Impromptu

For months now, I have been wandering
aimlessly. Endlessly.
A sweet deadly sunstroke
tortures and blinds me, night and day.

Where do these visitations come from?
Somebody steps from the water
dazzling, young,
slips through the abrupt darkness.

Her smile lifts toward the shore.
Far off, a few sails blaze.
The vertical noon heat
showers down on the litter of bathing huts.

Details and trivia.
A single flower in the soft wind
turning over and over, as in the fingers
of a mute and wondering baby.

And the melodies. Through all those rooms
the same wash of melodies,
as though the barefoot sea were roaming
among their walls.

But most beautiful of all – the lovers!
Their manes glowing out of the shadows
the last beautiful tent of their modesty.

The lovers. And the twilight.
The rows of houses, sinking into the dark.
And over the houses, on the sand,
a tower's ponderous mass.

Who could have dreamed up anything so sad?

[JC/TH]

Straight Labyrinth

How will it be, that flying back
of which only symbols tell –
altar, shrine, handshake,
homecoming, embrace,
table laid in the grass, under the trees,
where there is no first and no last guest –
how will it be, in the end how will it be
the wide-winged ascending plunge
back into the flaming
common nest of the focus? – I don't know,
and yet, if I know anything,
I know this – this hot corridor,
this labyrinth straight as an arrow
and fuller and fuller, freer and freer
the fact that we are flying.

[JC/TH]

Jewel

The antelope is looking at herself
in a perfectly-fashioned mirror.
Hanging at her neck: a gem.

Of her we say: beautiful as a tapestry.
We say: you just go on looking at yourself
and we shall bear children, be born, die.

We whisper things of this kind
to the antelope living in madness.

[JC/TH]

FERENC JUHÁSZ   1928–

Gold

The woman touches her bun
of thinning hair. She laughs,
and drops a spoon and a hunk of bread
in their reaching, grubby hands.
Like roses divining water
the circle of thin red necks
leans over the steaming plates;
red noses bloom in the savoury mist.

The stars of their eyes shine
like ten worlds lost in their own light.
In the soup, slowly circling
swim golden onion rings.

[DW]

Birth of the Foal

As May was opening the rosebuds,
elder and lilac beginning to bloom,
it was time for the mare to foal.
She'd rest herself, or hobble lazily

after the boy who sang as he led her
to pasture, wading through the meadowflowers.
They wandered back at dusk, bone-tired,
the moon perched on a blue shoulder of sky.

Then the mare lay down,
sweating and trembling, on her straw in the stable.
The drowsy, heavy-bellied cows
surrounded her, waiting, watching, snuffing.

Later, when even the hay slept
and the shaft of the Plough pointed south,

the foal was born. Hours the mare
spent licking the foal with its glue-blind eyes.

And the foal slept at her side,
a heap of feathers ripped from a bed.
Straw never spread as soft as this.
Milk or snow never slept like a foal.

Dawn bounced up in a bright red hat,
waved at the world and skipped away.
Up staggered the foal,
its hooves were jelly-knots of foam.

Then day sniffed with its blue nose
through the open stable window, and found them –
the foal nuzzling its mother,
velvet fumbling for her milk.

Then all the trees were talking at once,
chickens scrabbled in the yard,
like golden flowers
envy withered the last stars.

                    [DW]

Then There Are Fish

Forever confusing smoke with weeds,
clouds and sky with water.

Born with no lungs, just a blister
floating in a cage of splinters,
listless fins and hyperthyroid eyes.

Even the smallest fry
chase their hunger as boldly as carp –
mouths, nostrils, eyes
burst on a rising scream like a shoal of bubbles.

A world of nothing but water!

Houses and trees
float up like giant bubbles.

[DW]

Comet-watchers

One blind-calm summer night
someone tapped at the window of our house –
'Come out! Come out!
There's a miracle! There, in the sky!'

We jumped out of bed. What is it?
Some secret message from the stars?
I grabbed my mother's hand, it was warm,
I felt her heart beat in my palm.

Barefoot, in shirts and underpants
the whole village gathered out there in the cold;
scared old women, sleep-white faces
frozen in the white light of another world.

The poor came crowding into the street.
Women crossed their arms over their breasts.
Their knees shook as they gaped at the sky –
a fairy-tale, a holy prophecy!

Over the hill, the star-freaked sky
blazed brighter than burning hay –
a stallion with wings and a diamond mane,
a mane of fire, a streaming tail of blood.

I gripped my mother's hand like roots.
I remember the warmth of her body still,
and father pointing up at the horse
blazing away in the fires of its own sweat.

Proudly it flew away over the roofs.
We stood, still as gravestones in its fierce light.
The sky was much darker when it had gone.
O fate of comets, will o' the wisp, our hope!

[DW]

Mary

Like a little cow swollen with calf
she moons around the field, cow-eyed and staring.
The moon's silver belly hangs low in the sky,
the moon beginning to ebb, and the seas
ebbing with the moon.
She remembers the horde of children
locked in their room, shouting, their faces
pushed between the window-bars,
heads poking out to spy on the world,
red eyelids, petals of blood-red rose.
She loiters slowly away
like a little cow swollen with calf,
her rump swaying as she ambles along.
Above her the stars shine hard and cold.
Her heart-beats are too loud . . .
she doesn't understand . . . she stops,
looks down at her belly, and feels
the little feet kicking like a heart.

[DW]

GYÖRGY PETRI   1943–

'I am stuck, Lord, on your hook'

I am stuck, Lord, on your hook.
I've been wriggling there, curled up,
for the past twenty-six years,
alluringly, and yet
the line has never gone taut.
It's now clear
there are no fish in your river.
If you still have hopes, Lord, choose
another worm. It's been truly
beautiful,
being among the elect.
All the same, now I'd just like to
dry off, and loaf about in the sun.

                    [cw/gg]

Apocryphal

The holy family's grinding away –
Mary lies back, God screws;
Joseph, unable to sleep,
starts groping about for booze.
No luck: he gets up. Grabs his things.
Over pyjamas pulls vest and pants.
Then walks down to the Three Kings
for (at last!) a couple of pints . . .
'God again?'
                    'Him again.'
                              He sighs,
knocks back his beer, gets wise,
gesticulates:
                    'Anyway,
I can tell you, the other day
did I make a fuss: before my very eyes,

the two of 'em on the job!
So I told my Mary straight,
at least shut your gob,
it's enough that the damn bed shakes
and rumbles on as if there was an earthquake.
I mean it now: if he's really got to screw yuh,
I can do without all the ha-ha-ha-hallelujah!'

[CW/GG]

On the 24th Anniversary of the Little October Revolution

Uncle Imre, Uncle Pista and Co
corrected the world's course just a tiny bit.
They were hanged or locked up.
(Uncles Mátyás and Ernö buggered off
to Moscow. And the rest of them shall be nameless.)
Then came the land of Prester John:
'We'll never die!'
The total number of corpses –
and that includes both residents and intruders –
is estimated at somewhere between three thousand
and thirty thousand.
The figure is hard to verify so long
after the event. Many vanished.
Many were made to vanish.
Some people are put on the rack
of forgetlessness.
Some people were put on the rack.
Reality always reckons without herself.
Would she get her sums wrong? Settle her accounts?
A unified and indivisible entity
she failed her eleven-plus
has never properly learnt to count.
I say just two numbers:
56
68.
You can add them, subtract them,

divide or multiply.
Your innumerable doctrines, baseness is their basis,
have failed, are bankrupt.

[cw/gg]

Night Song of the Personal Shadow

The rain is pissing down,
you scum.
And you, you are asleep
in your nice warm room –
that or stuffing the bird.
Me? Till six in the morning
I rot in the slackening rain.
I must wait for my relief, I've got to wait
till you crawl out of your hole,
get up from beside your old woman.
So the dope can be passed on
as to where you've flown.
You are flying, spreading your wings.
Don't you get into my hands –
I'll pluck you while you're in flight.
This sodding rain
is something I won't forget,
my raincoat swelling
double its normal weight
and the soles of my shoes.
While you
were arsing around
in the warm room.

The time will come
when I feed you to fish in the Danube.

[cw/gg]

To Imre Nagy

You were impersonal, too, like the other leaders,
bespectacled, sober-suited; your voice lacked
sonority, for you didn't know quite what to say

on the spur of the moment to the gathered multitude. This urgency
was precisely the thing you found strange. I heard you,
old man in pince-nez, and was disappointed,
not yet to know

of the concrete yard where most likely the prosecutor
rattled off the sentence, or
of the rope's rough bruising, the ultimate shame.

Who can say what you might have said
from the balcony? Butchered opportunities
never return. Neither prison nor death
can resharpen the cutting edge of the moment

once it's been chipped. What we can do, though, is remember
the hurt, reluctant, hesitant man
who nonetheless soaked up
anger, delusion
and a whole nation's blind hope,

when the town awoke to gunfire
that blew it apart.

     [cw/gg]

Cold Peace

In the absence of peace, your plain man's mind might think:
there will be war. There being no war,
your learnèd mind would believe:
this now is peace. But it is and will be neither.

     [cw/gg]

Morning Coffee

I like the cold rooms of autumn, sitting
early in the morning at an open window,
or on the roof, dressing-gown drawn close,
the valley and the morning coffee glowing –
this cooling, that warming.

Red and yellow multiply, but the green
wanes, and into the mud the leaves
fall – fall in heaps,
the devalued currency of summer:
so much of it! so worthless!

Gradually the sky's
downy grey turns blue, the slight
chill dies down. The tide
of day comes rolling in –
in waves, gigantic, patient, barrelling.

I can start to carry on. I give myself up
to an impersonal imperative.

1986				[CW/GG]

SERBIA

VASKO POPA   1922—91

Pig

Only when she felt
The savage knife in her throat
Did the red veil
Explain the game
And she was sorry
She had torn herself
From the mud's embrace
And had hurried that evening
From the field so joyfully
Hurried to the yellow gate

                    [AP]

Before Play
To Zoran Mišić

One shuts one eye
Peers into oneself into every corner
Looks at oneself to see there are no spikes no thieves
No cuckoos' eggs

One shuts the other eye too
Crouches then jumps
Jumps high high high
To the top of oneself

Thence one drops by one's own weight
For days one drops deep deep deep
To the bottom of one's abyss

He who is not smashed to smithereens
He who remains whole and gets up whole
He plays

     [AP]

The Nail

One be the nail another the pincers
The others are workmen

The pincers take the nail by the head
With their teeth with their hands they grip him
And tug him tug
To get him out of the ceiling
Usually they only pull his head off
It's difficult to get a nail out of the ceiling

Then the workmen say
The pincers are no good
They smash their jaws they break their arms
And throw them out of the window

After that somone else be the pincers
Someone else the nail
The others are workmen

[AP]

The Seducer

One caresses the leg of a chair
Until the chair turns
And gives him a welcome sign with its leg

Another kisses a keyhole
Kisses it doesn't he just kiss it
Until the keyhole returns his kiss

A third stands by
Gapes at the other two
And twists his head twists it

Until his head falls off

[AP]

The Rose Thieves

Someone be a rose tree
Some be the wind's daughters
Some the rose thieves

The rose thieves creep up on the rose tree
One of them steals a rose
Hides it in his heart

The wind's daughters appear
See the tree plundered of its beauty
And give chase to the rose thieves

Open up their breasts one by one
In some they find a heart
In some so help me none

They go on opening up their breasts
Until they uncover one heart
And in that heart the stolen rose

[AP]

He

Some bite off the others'
Arm or leg or whatever

Take it between their teeth
Run off as quick as they can
Bury it in the earth

The others run in all directions
Sniff search sniff search
Turn up all the earth

If any are lucky enough to find their arm
Or leg or whatever
It's their turn to bite

The game goes on briskly

As long as there are arms
As long as there are legs
As long as there is anything whatever

[AP]

The Hunter

Someone goes in without knocking
Goes into somebody's one ear
And comes out of the other

Goes in with the step of a match
The step of a lighted match
Dances round inside his head

He's made it

Someone goes in without knocking
Goes into somebody's one ear
And doesn't come out of the other

He's done for

[AP]

Ashes

Some are nights others stars

Each night lights up its star
And dances a black dance round it
Until the star burns out

Then the nights split up
Some become stars
The others remain nights

Again each night lights up its star
And dances a black dance round it
Until the star burns out

The last night becomes both star and night
It lights itself
Dances the black dance round itself

[AP]

'Black be your tongue'

Black be your tongue black your noon black your hope
All be black only my horror white
My wolf be at your throat

The storm be your bed
My dread your pillow
Broad your unrest-field

Your food of fire your teeth of wax
Now chew you glutton
Chew all you want

Dumb be your wind dumb water dumb flowers
All be dumb only my gnashing aloud
My hawk be at your heart

Terror your mother be bereft

[AP]

'I've wiped your face off my face'

I've wiped your face off my face
Ripped your shadow off my shadow

Levelled the hills in you
Turned your plains into hills

Set your seasons at odds within you
Turned all the ends of the world from you

Wrapped the path of my life around you
My impenetrable my impossible path

Now you just try to find me

[AP]

Preparations for a Welcome

We set up a gate
Of our flowering bones
At the way into heaven

We spread half our soul
Up one slope of heaven

We devise a table
Of our petrified hands
At the very top of heaven

We spread half our soul
Down the other slope of heaven

We build a bed
Of our leafy heart
At the way out of heaven

We do all this in the dark
Alone without the help of time

We wonder if these are really
Preparations for a welcome
Or only for a farewell

[AP]

Midnight Sun

From a huge black egg
A sun was hatched to us

It shone on our ribs
It opened heaven wide
In our wretched breasts

It never set
But it never rose either

It turned everything in us gold
It turned nothing green
Around us around that gold

It changed into a tombstone
On our living heart

[AP]

GERMANY

PAUL CELAN   1920–70

Death Fugue

Black milk of daybreak we drink it at sundown
we drink it at noon in the morning we drink it at night
we drink and we drink it
we dig a grave in the breezes there one lies unconfined
A man lives in the house he plays with the serpents he writes
he writes when dusk falls to Germany your golden hair Margarete
he writes it and steps out of doors and the stars are flashing he
    whistles his pack out
he whistles his Jews out in earth has them dig for a grave
he commands us strike up for the dance

Black milk of daybreak we drink you at night
we drink in the morning at noon we drink you at sundown
we drink and we drink you
A man lives in the house he plays with the serpents he writes
he writes when dusk falls to Germany your golden hair Margarete
your ashen hair Shulamith we dig a grave in the breezes there one lies
    unconfined

He calls out jab deeper into the earth you lot you others sing now
    and play
he grabs at the iron in his belt he waves it his eyes are blue
jab deeper you lot with your spades you others play on for the dance

Black milk of daybreak we drink you at night
we drink you at noon in the morning we drink you at sundown
we drink and we drink you
a man lives in the house your golden hair Margarete
your ashen hair Shulamith he plays with the serpents

He calls out more sweetly play death death is a master from
    Germany
he calls out more darkly now stroke your strings then as smoke you
    will rise into air
then a grave you will have in the clouds there one lies unconfined

Black milk of daybreak we drink you at night
we drink you at noon death is a master from Germany
we drink you at sundown and in the morning we drink and we drink
    you
death is a master from Germany his eyes are blue
he strikes you with leaden bullets his aim is true
a man lives in the house your golden hair Margarete
he sets his pack on to us he grants us a grave in the air
he plays with the serpents and daydreams death is a master from
    Germany

your golden hair Margarete
your ashen hair Shulamith

                        [MH]

Think of it

Think of it:
the bog soldier of Massada
teaches himself home, most
inextinguishably,
against
every barb in the wire.

Think of it:
the eyeless with no shape
lead you free through the tumult, you
grow stronger and
stronger.

Think of it: your
own hand
has held
this bit of
habitable
earth, suffered up
again
into life.

Think of it:
this came towards me,
name-awake, hand-awake
for ever,
from the unburiable.

      [MH]

Psalm

No one moulds us again out of earth and clay,
no one conjures our dust.
No one.

Praised be your name, no one.
For your sake
we shall flower.
Towards
you.

A nothing
we were, are, shall
remain, flowering:
the nothing-, the
no one's rose.

With
our pistil soul-bright,
with our stamen heaven-ravaged,
our corolla red
with the crimson word which we sang
over, O over
the thorn.

      [MH]

Tenebrae

We are near, Lord,
near and at hand.

Handled already, Lord,
clawed and clawing as though
the body of each of us were
your body, Lord.

Pray, Lord,
pray to us,
we are near.

Askew we went there,
went there to bend
down to the trough, to the crater.

To be watered we went there, Lord.

It was blood, it was
what you shed, Lord.

It gleamed.

It cast your image into our eyes, Lord.
Our eyes and our mouths are so open and empty, Lord.
We have drunk, Lord.
The blood and the image that was in the blood, Lord.

Pray, Lord.
We are near.

[MH]

Homecoming

Snowfall, denser and denser,
dove-coloured as yesterday,
snowfall, as if even now you were sleeping.

White, stacked into distance.
Above it, endless,
the sleigh track of the lost.

Below, hidden,
presses up

what so hurts the eyes,
hill upon hill,
invisible.

On each,
fetched home into its today,
an I slipped away into dumbness:
wooden, a post.

There: a feeling,
blown across by the ice wind
attaching its dove-, its snow-
coloured cloth as a flag.

[MH]

Time's Eye

This is time's eye:
it squints out
from under a seven-hued eyebrow.
Its lid is washed clean by fires,
its tear is hot steam.

Towards it the blind star flies
and melts at the eyelash that's hotter:
it's growing warm in the world
and the dead
burgeon and flower.

[MH]

Nocturnally Pouting
For Hannah and Hermann Lenz

Nocturnally pouting
the lips of flowers,
criss-crossed and linked
the shafts of the spruces,
turned grey the moss, the stone shaken,

roused for unending flight
the jackdaws over the glacier:

this is the region where
those we've caught up with rest:

they will not name the hour,
they will not count the flakes
nor follow the stream to the weir.

They stand apart in the world,
each one close up to his night,
each one close up to his death,
surly, bare-headed, hoar-frosted
with all that is near, all that's far.

They discharge the guilt that adhered to their origin,
they discharge it upon a word
that wrongly subsists, like summer.

A word – you know:
a corpse.

Let us wash it,
let us comb it,
let us turn its eye
towards heaven.

[MH]

'Your hand full of hours'

Your hand full of hours, you came to me – and I said:
Your hair is not brown.
So you lifted it lightly on to the scales of grief; it weighed more than
      I . . .

On ships they come to you and make it their cargo, then put it on
      sale in the markets of lust –
You smile at me from the depth, I weep at you from the scale that
      stays light.

I weep: Your hair is not brown, they offer brine from the sea and you
    give them curls . . .
You whisper: They're filling the world with me now, in your heart
    I'm a hollow way still!
You say: Lay the leafage of years beside you – it's time you came
    closer and kissed me!

The leafage of years is brown, your hair is not brown.

[M H]

Sand from the Urns

Green as mould is the house of oblivion.
Before each of the blowing gates your beheaded minstrel turns blue.
For you he beats his drum made of moss and of harsh pubic hair;
With a festering toe in the sand he traces your eyebrow.
Longer he draws it than ever it was, and the red of your lip.
You fill up the urns here and nourish your heart.

[M H]

'Aspen tree, your leaves glance white'

Aspen tree, your leaves glance white into the dark.
My mother's hair was never white.

Dandelion, so green is the Ukraine.
My yellow-haired mother did not come home.

Rain cloud, above the well do you hover?
My quiet mother weeps for everyone.

Round star, you wind the golden loop.
My mother's heart was ripped by lead.

Oaken door, who lifted you off your hinges?
My gentle mother cannot return.

[M H]

Memory of France

Together with me recall: the sky of Paris, that giant autumn
    crocus . . .
We went shopping for hearts at the flower girl's booth:
they were blue and they opened up in the water.
It began to rain in our room,
and our neighbour came in, Monsieur Le Songe, a lean little man.
We played cards, I lost the irises of my eyes;
you lent me your hair, I lost it, he struck us down.
He left by the door, the rain followed him out.
We were dead and were able to breathe.

[MH]

Corona

Autumn eats its leaf out of my hand: we are friends.
From the nuts we shell time and we teach it to walk:
then time returns to the shell.

In the mirror it's Sunday,
in dream there is room for sleeping,
our mouths speak the truth.

My eye moves down to the sex of my loved one:
we look at each other,
we exchange dark words,
we love each other like poppy and recollection,
we sleep like wine in the conches,
like the sea in the moon's blood ray.

We stand by the window embracing, and people look up from the
    street:
it is time they knew!
It is time the stone made an effort to flower,
time unrest had a beating heart.
It is time it were time.

It is time.

[MH]

HANS MAGNUS ENZENSBERGER 1929–

for the grave of a peace-loving man

this one was no philanthropist,
avoided meetings, stadiums, the large stores.
did not eat the flesh of his own kind.

violence walked the streets,
smiling, not naked.
but there were screams in the sky.

people's faces were not very clear.
they seemed to be battered
even before the blow had struck home.

one thing for which he fought all his life,
with words, tooth and claw, grimly,
cunningly, off his own bat:

the thing which he called his peace,
now that he's got it, there is no longer a mouth
over his bones, to taste it with.

[MH]

a field of carnations

like your face, this thousand-leafed dawn
        your paleness
rows of mornings that open themselves
and i, who rejoice in everything measureless
        measure
the onset of darkness, fragrance of eyelashes
all these brief tremors
        flowering under the wind
and how can i help, how helpless, how
tell what fate shaped these air lanes
        for bats
how the bats fly how they fall

against the frail fields
    neuroses out of the sky
        the frail fields
    helpless to harm
    or to save
salvation for no one and nothing
and nobody's victims

      [jr]

vending machine

he puts four dimes into the slot
he gets himself some cigarettes

he gets cancer
he gets apartheid
he gets the king of greece
federal tax state tax sales tax and excise
he gets machine guns and surplus value
free enterprise and positivism
he gets a big lift big business big girls
the big stick the great society the big bang
the big puke
king size extra size super size

he gets more and more
for his four dimes
but for a moment all the things he is getting himself
disappear

even the cigarettes

he looks at the vending machine
but he doesn't see it
he sees himself
for a fleeting moment
and he almost looks like a man

then very soon he is gone again
with a little click
there are his cigarettes

he has disappeared
it was just a fleeting moment
some kind of sudden bliss

he has disappeared
he is gone
buried under all the stuff he has gotten
for his four dimes

joy

she does not want me to speak of her
she won't be put down on paper
she can't stand prophets

she is a stranger
but i know her
i know her well

she will overthrow all that is settled and fast
she will not lie
she will riot

by her alone i am justified
she is my reason, my reason of state
she does not belong to me

she is strange and headstrong
i harbour, i hide her
like a disgrace

she is a fugitive
not to be shared with others
not to be kept for yourself

i keep nothing from her
i share with her all i have
she will leave me

others will harbour her
on her long flight to victory
and hide her by night

Visiting Ingres

Today he'd be painting for the Central Committee, or Paramount,
it all depends. But at that time a gangster still sweated
under his ermine, and the con-men had themselves crowned.
So let's have them, the insignia, pearls, the peacock feathers.

We find the artist pensive. He has stuffed himself
with 'choice ideas and noble passions'.
A laborious business. Expensive small armchairs, First or Second
    Empire,
it all depends. Soft chin, soft hands, 'Hellas in his soul'.

For sixty years this cold greed, every inch a craftsman,
till he's achieved it: fame, the rosette in his buttonhole.

These women, writhing in front of him on the marble
like seals made of risen dough: 'between thumb and forefinger'
the breasts measured, the surface studied like plush,
tulle, glossy taffeta, the moisture in the corner of their eyes
glazed twelve times over like gelatine, the flesh colour smooth
and narcotic, better than Kodak: exhibited
in the Ecole des Beaux-Arts, a venal eternity.

What's it all for? What for the tin of his decorations,
the fanatical industry, the gilt plaster eagles?

Curiously bloated he looks at eighty,
worn out, with that top hat in his left hand.
'It was all for nothing'. How can you say that, most honoured
    Maître!
What will the frame-maker think of you, the glazier,
your faithful cook, the undertaker? His only answer:
A sigh. Far above the clouds, oneiric, the fingers of Thetis
that squirm like worms on Jupiter's black beard.
Reluctantly we take a last brief look

at the artist – how short his legs are! –
and tiptoe out of the studio.

[MH]

The Divorce

At first it was only an imperceptible quivering of the skin –
'As you wish' – where the flesh is darkest.
'What's wrong with you?' – Nothing. Milky dreams
of embraces; next morning, though,
the other looks different, strangely bony.
Razor-sharp misunderstandings. 'That time, in Rome –'
I never said that. A pause. And furious palpitations,
a sort of hatred, strange. 'That's not the point.'
Repetitions. Radiantly clear, this certainty:
From now on all is wrong. Odourless and sharp,
like a passport photo, this unknown person
with a glass of tea at table, with staring eyes.
It's no good, no good, no good:
litany in the head, a slight nausea.
End of reproaches. Slowly the whole room
Fills with guilt right up to the ceiling.
This complaining voice is strange, only not
the shoes that drop with a bang, not the shoes.
Next time, in an empty restaurant,
slow motion, bread crumbs, money is discussed,
laughing – The dessert tastes of metal.
Two untouchables. Shrill reasonableness.
'Not so bad really.' But at night
the thoughts of vengeance, the silent fight, anonymous
like two bony barristers, two large crabs
in water. Then the exhaustion. Slowly
the scab peels off. A new tobacconist,
a new address. Pariahs, horribly relieved.
Shades growing paler. These are the documents.
This is the bunch of keys. This is the scar.

[MH]

The Force of Habit

I
Ordinary people ordinarily do not care
for ordinary people.
And vice versa.
Ordinary people find it extraordinary
that people find them extraordinary.
At once they have ceased to be ordinary.
And vice versa.

II
That one gets used to everything –
one gets used to that.
The usual name for it is
a learning process.

III
It is painful
when the habitual pain does not present itself.
How tired the lively mind
is of its liveliness!
The simple person there for instance finds it complicated
to be a simple person,
while that complex character
rattles off his complexity
as nuns do their rosaries.
All these eternal beginners
who long ago reached the end.
Hatred, too, is a precious habit.

IV
The utterly unprecedented –
we are used to that.
The utterly unprecedented
is our habitual right.
A creature of habit
at the usual corner meets
an habitual criminal.
An unheard-of occurrence.

The usual shit.
Our 'classics' were in the habit
of turning it into stories.

v
Untroubled the habit of force reposes
on the force of habit.

[MH]

Concert of Wishes

Samad says: Give me my daily pita
Fräulein Brockmann looks for a comfortable little flat not too
  expensive with a cooking recess and a broom cupboard
Véronique longs for world revolution
Dr Luhmann desperately needs to sleep with his mama
Uwe Köpke dreams of a perfect specimen of Thurn and Taxis seven
  silber-groschen pale blue imperforated
Simone knows exactly what she wants: to be famous Simply famous
  no matter for what or at what price
If Konrad had his way he'd simply lie in bed for ever
Mrs Woods would like to be tied up and raped quite regularly but
  only from behind and by a gentleman
Guido Ronconi's only desire is the *unio mystica*
Fred Podritzke would love to work over all those crackpot Lefties
  with a length of gas piping until not one of them so much as
  twitches
If someone doesn't give him his steak and chips this minute Karel
  will blow his top
What Buck needs is a flash and nothing else

And peace on earth and a ham sandwich and the undirected
  dialogue
    and a baby and a million free of tax and a moaning that gives
    way to the familiar little breathless shrieks and a plush
    poodle and freedom for all and off with his head and that the
    hair we have lost will grow again overnight

[MH]

SWEDEN

TOMAS TRANSTRÖMER 1931–

Morning Approach

The black-backed gull, the sun-captain, holds his course.
Beneath him is the water.
The world is still sleeping like a
multicoloured stone in the water.
Undeciphered day. Days –
like aztec hieroglyphs.

The music. And I stand trapped
in its Gobelin weave with
raised arms – like a figure
out of folk art.

    [RF]

Tracks

2 a.m.: moonlight. The train has stopped
out in the middle of the plain. Far away, points of light in a town,
flickering coldly at the horizon.

As when a man has gone into a dream so deep
he'll never remember having been there
when he comes back to his room.

As when someone has gone into an illness so deep
everything his days were becomes a few flickering points, a swarm,
cold and tiny at the horizon.

The train is standing quite still.
2 a.m.: bright moonlight, few stars.

    [RF]

Winter's Formulae

I
I fell asleep in my bed
and woke up under the keel.

At four o'clock in the morning
when life's clean picked bones
coldly associate with each other.

I fell asleep among the swallows
and woke up among the eagles.

II
In the lamplight the ice on the road
is gleaming like lard.

This is not Africa.
This is not Europe.
This is nowhere other than 'here'.

And that which was 'I'
is only a word
in the December dark's mouth.

III
The institute's pavilions
displayed in the dark
shine like TV screens.

A hidden tuning-fork
in the great cold
sends out its tone.

I stand under the starry sky
and feel the world creep
in and out of my coat
as in an ant-hill.

IV
Three dark oaks out of the snow.
So gross, but nimble-fingered.

Out of their giant bottles
the greenery will bubble in spring.

V

The bus crawls through the winter evening.
It glimmers like a ship in the spruce forest
where the road is a narrow deep dead canal.

Few passengers: some old and some very young.
If it stopped and quenched the lights
the world would be deleted.

[RF]

Alone

I

One evening in February I came near to dying here.
The car skidded sideways on the ice, out
on the wrong side of the road. The approaching cars –
their lights – closed in.

My name, my girls, my job
broke free and were left silently behind
further and further away. I was anonymous
like a boy in a playground surrounded by enemies.

The approaching traffic had huge lights.
They shone on me while I pulled at the wheel
in a transparent terror that floated like egg white.
The seconds grew – there was space in them –
they grew big as hospital buildings.

You could almost pause
and breathe out for a while
before being crushed.

Then something caught: a helping grain of sand
or a wonderful gust of wind. The car broke free
and scuttled smartly right over the road.
A post shot up and cracked – a sharp clang – it
flew away in the darkness.

Then – stillness. I sat back in my seat-belt
and saw someone coming through the whirling snow
to see what had become of me.

II

I have been walking for a long time
on the frozen Östergötland fields.
I have not seen a single person.

In other parts of the world
there are people who are born, live and die
in a perpetual crowd.

To be always visible – to live
in a swarm of eyes –
a special expression must develop.
Face coated with clay.

The murmuring rises and falls
while they divide up among themselves
the sky, the shadows, the sand grains.

I must be alone
ten minutes in the morning
and ten minutes in the evening.
– Without a programme.

Everyone is queuing at everyone's door.

Many.

One.

[RF]

A Few Minutes

The squat pine in the swamp holds up its crown: a dark rag.
But what you see is nothing
compared to the roots, the widespread, secretly creeping, immortal
    or half-mortal
root-system.

I you she he also branch out.
Outside what one wills.
Outside the Metropolis.

A shower falls out of the milk-white summer sky.
It feels as if my five senses were linked to another creature
which moves stubbornly
as the brightly-clad runners in a stadium where the darkness streams
    down.

[RF]

To Friends behind a Frontier

I

I wrote so meagrely to you. But what I couldn't write
swelled and swelled like an old-fashioned airship
and drifted away at last through the night sky.

II

The letter is now at the censor's. He lights his lamp.
In the glare my words fly up like monkeys on a grille,
rattle it, stop, and bare their teeth.

III

Read between the lines. We'll meet in 200 years
when the microphones in the hotel walls are forgotten
and can at last sleep, become trilobites.

[RF]

FINLAND

At Grand Opera

Through the ox-eye the drama's mere pantomime
here in the gods at the opera house where passion flares:
far down in the earth's stalls the audience sits
stiff as silver foil in a smoke of voices.

The bloodshot eye sees in a world-stage action
only this unheard voice from the grave of grimaces
that climbs to us near the space-roof's smooth arch
to hear what we couldn't hear from unknown agony,

and to waver in wind-currents no one has felt
except one giddily watching who sees his life
realized at a distance, near the abyss
and hear's humanity's voice like a glissando in darkness.

[AB]

'Removal vans drew children like ambulances'

Removal vans drew children like ambulances.
Everything looked poorer in the merciless light.
The flower-pots like a final greeting to the obsequies of intimacies,
beds, bedclothes, contorted chairs:
everything crouched under a shroud that came too late.
We were caught out! But we discovered things too:
empty rooms where we'd lived, grease-spots behind the tapestry
and the scratched floors, the gas-cooker rusting away.
Deprived of a room the spirit crouched, given
over to shoddy things whose warmth no one could see.
I jolted along on the front of the load, I was
born a lodger.

[AB]

'You had to watch out'

You had to watch out not to step on lines, spit at cats,
walk under ladders, run upstairs two at a time
till you were panting after release from self-imposed torture.
The kitchen tablecloth had its maddening pattern.
There were always rules. The exceptions were like summer
    swallows,
rare sweeping cries soon gone
and the courtyard quiet as Sunday.
The rules were there to make life more secret than it was.
And thoughts moved hushed as a shuttle
and wove the most intricate webs
or wondrous colours.

[AB]

'For a moment they stand out'

For a moment they stand out but mostly they're faceless.
They wear a peaked cap and a hard shadow or narrow legs
that take them out into the street and on past dizzy heights
down to the sea and the Russian church and the houses where only
    the dead live.
They're sprinkled like seed and buried among old houses
and come up gasping for air in the dark where a few lamps
rock and strike against patterned plaster walls with black iron.
There pale girls grab them, tough as their voices,
have swarms of children and move with big mattresses
to smaller rooms where coughs and joblessness live snug.
On early misty mornings when spring rises from the sea
and the children have stormed from the nest they sit with long still
    hands
and watch us playing, if they see us at all, they're buried
in wear and tear, overlong raincoats, their stubble silver-white.
Later they're just not there.
They probably lived in the same place for forty years,
and walked along streets and in through dark portals
where suddenly no one was in.

Those days when they're borne away are always in mind
shrouded in chimney smoke.

[AB]

'When you drive up to the four-star pump'

When you drive up to the four-star pump
there's always another car, grubby, empty,
just standing there, God knows where its owner is.
The registration number shows he's a local.
By the self-service pump: no one.
It's dirty and cold, strip lighting here too,
and a deafening drill blocks your ears,
digs a pit for a new tank.

At the cash point you can buy
sweets, cassettes, porn mags, condoms
and, tanked up, oil-filled, with a clean windscreen
drive out into the dark landscape
before one of the gang hanging round outside
grabs hold of the door and staggering, with a face
pale as paper, yells something
you can't catch, which scares you
or fills you with rage, later
when you're alone on the road, and the radio's
playing wonderful clear Vivaldi.

[AB]

Old Man

He turns his life inwards to the courtyard. It is dark.
He was born in the century that blew away
and sees how something forgotten
rises and falls like waves of asphalt.
The sunlight strikes him like a blow.
Someone braced his foot against a breast

and pulled out the bayonet, blood came streaming
warm, thick, like oil.
It darkened before his eyes and stayed there,
the men lay on the scorched slope,
swallows whooped over the roof, their screams swift as shadows.
Twenty years old, overgrown, the second birth,
the woman's averted eyes
forced him into himself, just as he
forced himself into her.
The rest was work, poverty, stone
as long as stone was needed.
So people fade, die.
The years rose in him, like marsh water.
The third birth: into the silence, the backyard Sunday,
unreal, waiting, a wisp of smoke,
unseen.

[AB]

Address

Take the left escalator
go through Gate B
take the moving walkway to Platform 7
entrain to the Central Mall
take the subway under the clearway
then the footbridge to the pedestrian level.
Continue through the arcades.
Turn at the Heelbar and head via the Disco
for Automatic Exit A.
Just beyond the Piazza
you'll see twelve high-rises
lining both sides of Seawind Street.
Veer left down Loganberry Lane
to Reddle Cottage
third left past the Samarkand Restaurant.
Look for Entrance M just opposite the Waste Disposal Lot
and take the express lift to the top floor.
From Level 14 it's two flights to the penthouse,

where you'll find a door painted blue, no name on it.
Knock, to be on the safe side.
That's where I live doing my job
of painting the sky.
You can give me a hand if you like.

[HL]

'Here is a field with spring dew'

Here is a field with spring dew,
an outlook south, a cloud
that pauses, moves on, pauses
like a heavy waggon.
The light comes and goes on the roads, the roads
that are driven threadbare
as if they had carried all of life's lumber.
Sunlight glitters on water gathered
in the winding tracks of the clay
but quickly fades.
You take a step or two towards the dark wall.
The cold wind scarcely moves the trees.
Darkness arrives as if it rose
out of the ground and surrounded you,
stooped over you as once the mother
stooped over her child
lowering it in sleep.

[BC/RF]

'As we started on our way up'

As we started on our way up we noticed
there were no windows facing west,
facing forest and sea – we asked the owner:
demolition, wall standing against wall,
what was invisible then was visible now,
there was a view, if we'd just follow him.
We began that endless climb

in the dark spiral stairway with its worn treads.
We felt ourselves grow older the higher we got,
and short of breath – what was this, a light-house?
It was meant to be a house to live in.
At the top this man we didn't know and saw
obscurely in the darkness we'd taken with us
opened an iron door. A white-washed hall,
embrasures and peep-holes, a view of straits,
of wide forests, in the bays white sails
and, deep down, trees moving slowly.
As if they wanted to show us something, or warn us.
We looked west. The sun was sinking, a glow spread
on a tin roof, a child-like church-bell rang.
The man who's led us here was almost black against the light.

[BC/RF]

'The bees that increase and diminish'

The bees that increase and diminish their persistent singing
increase and diminish the heat too – their fury
blocks the sky's windows, divides the ground into shadow and sun.
Rest on such a day is confused, in your dream
the room is locked and you'll never find the key –
the number's forgotten. The sun slowly enters clouds.
Silence, like a graveyard of the winds
where each thinning stem stands with its back to you
hiding the twisting path. You didn't think
that dusk would fall so quickly?
You thought someone would meet you before nightfall?
Years are forgotten – you leave no tracks and listen no more
even to the echo of songs from black thickets.
When you waken you look at the window.
The vehement light there is itself a token of darkness.

[BC/RF]

'Mile after mile the roots go'

Mile after mile the roots go, underground,
the meadow rests greenly, then withers
and foliage decays, roads
run through the dark,
the roots reach so deep, petrify,
make their way in to the cities,
asphalt rises and cracks,
in great heat a shadow is burnt
on the wall that took root –

the roots entwine themselves,
what those who see call the crown
those who know call the root,
its sap flows like a dark river
through sunlit branches,
roots move to and fro up there
in the wind that sweeps
across the city roofs and spires,
out towards the sea, the speechless depths.

[BC/RF]

PAAVO HAAVIKKO   1931–

from The Short Year

I light the candles each side of the winter chrysanthemums.
    I see you, your fingers splayed, counting on your fingers.
I know what you're counting: the months.
    Soon you'll talk about it.
The fingers that make you a door are now
    occupied so abstractly.
A short year, so short that at the year's end
    you'll be hugging a three-month baby;
or like a man's life, a year, and the second snow
    has already fallen without his making a single print.
Death comes abruptly to a man. A woman makes her death
    little by little, makes children,
and her happiness is to die before they do.
    When she weeps for a child, her voice and her flesh are one.

                        [. . .]

Leaves want to dance, and they get wind and storm,
    · and autumn days, suddenly calm, and open;
and if the pines started to shed needles
    you'd not dare query was it always so every autumn.
Nights. As only softness can be cruel,
    her soft childlike features are showing
a furious face. Her names are Nightbeauty,
    Softness, Always, Two-Shallow-Hollows,
Dimple-In-The-Pelvis-Just-Above-The-Thighs, and
    Two-Just-Near-The-Spine, as if someone had
just pressed them there with his hands,
    That-Smiling-Absentminded-Look,
The-Look-That-Comes-When-A-Hand-Is-Drawn-From-A-Glove.

                        [. . .]

Warmer than the air around her,
              cooler than the waiting water,
    she dawdles long, alone in the room,
                        without dressing,
as she's nothing to take off.
Awful to see such great despair, so few gestures.

[HL]

from Poems from the House of a Novgorod Merchant

The male seeks himself, woman, God, the tribe, age, the grave.
    A seeker, unappeasable by less.
Twins, half a person, a single fate, firm proof
    that a person is composed before his birth.

[. . .]

Woman, dreamstuff, meat that's sweet,
    spun manically, hastily from dusk,
to be done when the dream brings the male,
    knitted from twigs, gathered from the wind, fast walking.

[. . .]

I dreamed of a man who was out to do me in a deal.
    Out to give me counterfeit money –
a counterfeit king's counterfeit money!
    But luckily for me, my goods are rotten,
rotted in transport. He was blind with greed
    and snapped them up, the goods.
Rotten money for rancid goods.
    Not a bad deal for me.

For better a pig in a poke than bad stock
    that nobody wants.
With bad stock, you can't go to law, seek justice,
    but with a criminal merchant you can.

[. . .]

So alone. That, as the only jewel
                           on her breasts,
        she raises her arm, scratching her neck.
The hand is someone else, the neck someone else's.
        Self-deception.
She, her hand, arm, breasts, throat, neck and her scratching
                                   are an intaglio depicting
that a woman suckles not a child but a fate.

                           [HL]

from In the World

I vote for spring, autumn gets in, winter forms the cabinet.
Tell me whose lot you stand with, whose songs you sing
        with your mouth full of glass.
I'm against socialism, capitalism, its, their crimes.
I'm against their crimes, I swear, I share in them.

                           [. . .]

The best of man is his short duration,
                           that he disappears
        once and for all.
Dead from the world's foundation
                           till his birth,
        why should he wake up to do things
that'll last for ever?

                           [. . .]

When the bad lady wants your promotion, colonel,
        she wants you posted — after your house, general.
When your TB's getting terminal, it's lysol for you
        as your cough mixture.
A man a dictator only saved with difficulty
        from his own oppression
became a showpiece people came miles to see.
        Drowned himself.

A woman who rushed with her children
    onto a Jewish extermination train
left nothing but ash, colonel, ash and a widower.
    A man who refused to tell the story to the end.
He was eliminated. Look around you. Why should I go on?

[. . .]

In debt for goose eggs, don't take a loan for duck eggs.
When the rate's ten per cent, it draws gold down from the moon.
When they're buying, sell. Buy when they're selling.
First think slowly, then act quickly.
Get out of bad businesses fast.
    Forget them.
A hundred years from now this is a hundred years ago.
Never be afraid of the obvious.

[. . .]

The seedlings, the firs, need your help through the grass.
    For a year or two, perhaps five, they're grateful.
Then the grass needs your help to survive the trees.
    It goes bald round them,
                 around their majesty.
And the pine that grew fifteen years in an alder grove,
    three feet high, sinuous, bowed, bent with snow,
        starts to prosper.
It kills everything within reach
    for the next two hundred years, annually.
That's where it has to be.
    Never say it's growing in the wrong place,
    a tree.

[HL]

[. . .]

I have seen eyes that have seen a man
    whose eyes have seen eyes
that have seen eyes that have seen
                seen Stalin
whose eyes have seen eyes
    that have seen Hitler

who has seen eyes that have seen the Kaiser
    whose eyes have seen Victoria
who has seen eyes that have seen
                seen eyes
    that have seen the man
who has seen the sources of the Nile, the man, the eyes,
    India, elephants, Alexander, Antioch,
hippopotamus and crocodile.

And that man is truly venerable because
    he always lived in the same world
as the hippopotamus.

[. . .]

The world has always been a terrible place,
                beautiful and expensive.
Female flesh has always been worth its weight
    a mighty fixer of prices, a power of many intrigues.
Death is greedy, it takes away from me all the trees,
    one by one; sight, hearing.

[. . .]

This is a world that will, in any case, be destroyed at some time.
Working for its destruction seems pointless.
    It is impossible to save. Between these two facts, life has to be
lived.
    Other creatures, human and divine, differ from the mouse
only by the frequency of their breath-rate
    in and out, quickly, until you lose it.
    Now, the universe is breathing out: a great breath, so that,
from inside, it looks slow, and distant, from this edge.
    When it starts breathing in, it will have breathed only once: out,
and in.
    It's time to stop recycling waste paper, it is time to stop
producing it.
You are told that it, too, is an industry that uses up energy
    so what's it matter what you do?

And who am I if not industry and war, destruction and
waste? I should write smaller, tell fewer lies,
    get it all said, should lower my voice.

[AH]

from May, Perpetual

Poetry is no season
           or weather:
   it's a climate;
no place, no landscape but
    an all-purpose economy and history
in a single house.
    A passion larger than life.
Masoned so that however many
    it's masoned from,
        it shows no seams.
The seams are all in sight,
    the different stones one slab.

[. . .]

When the soul seizes power,
    the mind makes it the heir,
imitates a musical box
    itself always listening
     and astonished
that a mechanical nightingale has
    a nightingale's lot,
     a marsh warbler's:
        to concoct, echo
    and coax the whole clutch of voices
      into its voice

[HL]

from Ten Poems from the Year 1966

The round moon phase now seems to last longer than before.
Women, endlessly as hair in their hairdos
        walk in the streets,
in the streets, destinies,
            hairdos, tight on both sides of the head
                        the coifed hair,
women, hairdos, certain streets where they walk
        always turning like the lines of their hair.
Women, like hair, sorrows, like hair, endlessly.

                        [. . .]

A round moon, a woman undressing, flowing vertical water,
        night comes.
The moon moves faster than the thin clouds.
The moon moves faster than the thin clouds when the cold
                        begins to reveal the sky.
The moon moves faster than the thin clouds,
                            the woman
        walks through the cold room, shedding her clothes
as she goes through the room, and the room is cold.
        She is in a hurry to get under the covers.
The moon moves faster than the thin clouds.

                        [AH]

ITALY

GIUSEPPE UNGARETTI   1888–1970

Day by Day
1940–46

1
'No one, mother, has ever suffered so . . .'
And the face already dead
But still the living eyes
Turned from the pillow towards the window,
And sparrows filled the room
Coming for the crumbs the father scattered
To distract his child . . .

2
Now only in dreams will I be able
To kiss those trusting hands . . .
And I talk, I work,
I've scarcely changed, I smoke, I am afraid . . .
How is it I stand up to so much night? . . .

3
The years will bring me
God knows what other horrors,
But if I felt you by me
You would console me . . .

4
Never, you will never know how it fills me with light,
The shade that comes and stands beside me, shyly,
When I no longer hope . . .

5
Where is it now, where is the innocent voice
That running and resounding from room to room
Raised a tired man from his troubles? . . .
The earth has spoilt it, it is protected by
A past of fairytales . . .

6
Every other voice is a fading echo
Now that one voice calls me
From the immortal heights . . .

7
In the sky I seek your happy face,
And may these eyes of mine see nothing else
When God wills it that they too shall close . . .

8
And I love you, love you, and it is an endless wrenching! . . .

9
Ferocious earth, monstrous sea
Divide me from the place where the grave is
Where that tormented body
Now wastes away . . .
It doesn't matter . . . Ever more distinctly
I hear that voice of soul
That I failed to succour here below . . .
More joyful and more friendly
As the minutes pass,
It isolates me in its simple secret . . .

10
I have gone back to the hills, to the beloved pines,
And the homely accent of the wind's rhythm
That I will hear no more with you
Breaks me with every gust . . .

11
The swallow passes and summer with her
And I too, I tell myself, will pass . . .
But of the love that rends me may some sign
Remain, apart from this brief misting-over,
If from this hell I reach some kind of peace . . .

12
Under the axe the disenchanted branch
Falls with scarcely a complaint, less
Even than the leaf at the breeze's touch . . .

And it was fury that cut down the tender
Form, and the eager
Compassion of a voice consumes me . . .

13
Summer brings me no more furies,
Nor spring its forebodings;
You can go your way, autumn
With your idiot splendours:
For a desire stripped bare, winter
Extends the gentlest season! . . .

14
Already the drought of autumn
Has sunk into my bones,
But, drawn out by the shadows,
There survives an endless
Demented splendour:
The secret torment of the twilight buried
In an abyss . . .

15
Will I always recall without remorse
A bewitching agony of the senses?
Blind man, listen: 'A spirit has departed
Still unharmed by the common lash of life . . .'

Will I be less cast down to hear no more
The living cries of his innocence
Than to feel almost dead in me
The dreadful shudder of guilt?

16
In the dazzle blaring from the windows
Shade frames a reflection on the tablecloth,
In the faint lustre of a jar the swollen
Hydrangeas from the flower-bed, a drunken swift,
The skyscraper in a blaze of clouds,
A child rocking on a bough, return to mind . . .
Inexhaustible thunder of the waves
Forces upon me then, invades the room

And, on the uneasy stillness of a blue
Horizon, all the walls dissolve . . .

17
Mild weather, and perhaps you pass close by
Saying: 'May this sun and so much space
Calm you. In the pure wind you can hear
Time walking, and my voice.
Little by little I have closed and gathered
The mute impulse of your hope in me.
For you I am the dawn and the unbroken day.'

[PC]

A series of fragments written at various times after the death of the poet's
nine-year-old son in 1939. (*Translator's note*)

Bitter Chiming

Or else on an October afternoon
From the harmonious hills
Amongst thick lowering clouds
The horses of the Heavenly Twins,
At whose hoofs a boy
Had paused enchanted,
Over storm-water launched

(By a bitter chiming of memories
Towards shadows of banana trees
And of giant turtles
Lumbering between masses
Of vast impassive waters:
Under a different order of stars
Among unfamiliar seagulls)

Their flight to the level place where the boy
Rummaging in the sand –
The transparency of his beloved fingers
Wet with driven rain
Turned to flame by splendour of the lightning –
Clutched all four elements.

But death is colourless and without senses
And ignorant of any law, as ever,
Already grazed him
With its shameless teeth.

[PC]

You Were Broken

1
The many grey, monstrous, scattered stones
Still shuddering in the hidden slings
Of stifled primal flames
Or in the terrors of virgin floods
Crumbling in implacable embraces,
– Don't you remember them, on a void horizon
Rigid above the dazzle of the sand?

And leaning, and spreading at the only
Meeting-place of shade in the whole valley,
The monkey-puzzle, breathless, overbloated,
Wound in the arduous flint of lonely fibres,
More stubborn even than the other damned,
Its mouth cool with butterflies and grasses
Where it tore itself from its own roots,
– Don't you remember it, delirious mute
Upon a rounded stone one foot across
In perfect balance
Magically there?

From branch to branch light firecrest
Avid eyes drunk with wonder
You reached its dappled peak,
Reckless one, child of music,
Only to see once more in the last light
Of a deep still sea-chasm
Legendary turtles
Stirring amongst the seaweed.
Nature's utmost tension

And underwater pageants,
Funereal warnings.

2
You raised your arms like wings
And gave rebirth to the wind
Running in the heaviness of the still air.

No one ever saw you rest
Your light dancer's foot.

3
Grace, happy thing,
In such a hardened blindness
How could you not be broken?
You, simple breath and crystal,

A flash of light too human for the savage,
Pitiless, frenzied, throbbing
Roar of a naked sun.

[PC]

In My Veins

Desire still riding hard in my veins
That by now are almost empty tombs,
In my freezing bones the stone,
In my spirit the dumb lament,
Invincible iniquity: dissolve them.

From remorse, howl without end,
In the unutterable dark
Claustral terror,
Redeem me, raise
Your merciful lashes from your long sleep.

Engendering mind, raise once more
Your rose-coloured unexpected sign,
And take me by surprise again.
Unhoped for, yet arise
O unbelievable dimension, peace;

In the soaring landscape make it so
That I may once more spell out simple words.

[PC]

Cry Out No More

Stop killing the dead,
Cry out no more, do not cry out
If you wish still to hear them,
If you hope not to perish.

Their whisper is imperceptible,
They make no more noise
Than the growth of grass,
Happy where no man passes.

[PC]

Variations on Nothing

That nothing nothingness of sand that runs
Dumbly from the hourglass and sifts down,
And, momentary, the imprints on the flesh,
On the dying complexion, of a cloud . . .

Then a hand that turns the hourglass over,
The return, the stirring, of the sand,
The unsounded silvering of a cloud
At the first brief glimmerings of dawn . . .

The hand, in shadow, turned the hourglass over,
And that nothingness of sand running
Silently, is all we can still hear,
And that, being heard, does not go down to darkness.

[PC]

EUGENIO MONTALE   1896–1981

The Storm

Les princes n'ont point d'yeux pour voir ces grands merveilles,
Leurs mains ne servent plus qu'à nous persécuter . . .
                                 Agrippa D'Aubigné: 'A Dieu'

The storm that pelts the tough leaves
of the magnolia with long
March thunders, with hailstones,

(crystal sounds in your nighttime
nest startle you; what's left of the gold
doused on the mahogany, on the tooling
of bound books, still burns
a grain of sugar in the shell
of your eyelids)

the lightning blaze that candies
trees and walls surprising them in this
forever of an instant – marble, manna
and destruction – which you bear carved
inside you, your condemnation, and lashes
you to me, strange sister, more than love –
and then the rough crash, rattles, thrill of
timbrels over the hidden pit,
the stamp of the fandango, and beyond it
some groping gesture . . .

                        The way it was when
you turned, and with your hand brushed
from your forehead a cloud of hair,

and waved to me – and stepped into darkness.

                    [SR/AP]

In Sleep

The cries of screech-owls, or the intermittent heartbeats
of dying butterflies,
or the tossing and turning
sighs of the young, or the bald error that tightens
like a garrote around the temples, or the vague horror
of upturned cedars in the onrush of sleep – all this
can come back to me, overflowing from ditches,
bursting from waterpipes, and make me wide awake
to your voice. The music of a slow, demented dance
cuts through; the enemy clangs down
his visor, hiding his face. The amaranth moon
enters behind the closed eyelids, becomes a swelling
cloud; and when sleep takes it
deeper in, it is still blood beyond any death.

[cw]

The Strands of Hair . . .

Don't push back the strands of hair which veil
your child-like forehead. They, too, speak
of you – they are the whole sky wherever I go,
my only light except for the jades
which circle your wrist; in the riot
of sleep they drop like curtains, bringing
your amnesties; they carry you,
transmigratory Artemis, unharmed
among the blood-baths of the still-born; and, if now
hair light as down flowers
upon that brow, you, come down from some height,
alter its color, your restless forehead
covers the dawn, and hides it.

[cw]

To My Mother

Now that the chorus of the rock partridge
lulls you in the eternal sleep and the gay,
broken band is in flight toward the hills
of Mesco, long picked clean of their harvest; now that the struggle
of the living rages even stronger, if you yield up,
like a shadow, your last remains
                    (and it isn't a shadow,
it isn't kind – it isn't what you think)
who will protect you? The cleared highway
is not a passage; only two hands, a face,
those hands, *that* face, the gestures of a life
that is nothing but itself –
only this puts you into the heaven
thick with the souls and voices that you live by;

and the question you leave unanswered is also
only a gesture in the shadow of the crosses.

                                [cw]

Ballad Written in a Clinic

In the furrow of emergency:

when the lunatic comet of August
was loosed beyond the mountains
in the still serene air

– but darkness, for us, and terror,
bridges and belvederes collapsing
above us, buried deep, like Jonah
in the belly of the whale –

I turned away and the mirror
said I was not the same
because the throat and the chest
of a chalk mannequin
had suddenly encased you.

In the deep sockets of your eyes
shone lenses of tears
thicker than your heavy
tortoiseshell glasses
which I remove at night and place
next to the vials of morphine.

The bull-god was not ours, but
the God who ignites
the lilies in the ditch:
I summoned Aries and the horned
beast's passage swept away
the last shreds of pride, even the heart
cracked from your coughing.

I wait for a sign that the hour
of final abduction is near:
I am ready, and penitence
begins then, a hollow
weeping from the peaks and valleys
of the *other* emergency.

On your bureau you kept
the wooden bulldog, the alarm-clock
with the phosphorus hands
which shed a tenuous splendor
on your drowsings, half-awake,

the nothingness – enough for those
who mean to force the narrow gate;
outside now, red on white,
a cross hoists and unfurls.

With you I turn toward the voice
which breaks in the dawn, the enormous
presence of the dead; the soundless howl

of the wooden dog is mine.

[DY/VR]

The Hitler Spring

The dense white cloud of the mayflies crazily
Whirls around the pallid street lamps and over the parapets,
Spread on the ground a blanket on which the foot
Grates as on sprinkled sugar; the looming summer now
Releases the nightfrosts which it was holding
In the secret caves of the dead season,
In the gardens of Maiano where the sandpits stop.

And soon over the street an infernal messenger passes in flight;
The murderers salute; a mystical gulf, fired
And beflagged with swastikas, has taken and swallowed us;
The shopwindows, humble and inoffensive, are closed
Though armed – they also –
With cannon and toys of war;
The butcher has struck who dresses with flowers and berries
The muzzles of the slaughtered goats.
The ritual of the mild hangman, once innocent of blood,
Is changed to a spastic dance of shattering wings,
The mayflies' tiny deaths whiten the piers' edge
And the water continues to eat at the
Shoreline, and no one is any more blameless.

All for nothing, then? – and the Roman candles
At San Giovanni, which gradually
Blanched the horizon, and the pledges and the long farewells
Strong as a baptism, in the sorrowful expectation
Of the horde, (but a bud striped the air, distilling
On the ice and on the rivers of your country
The messengers of Tobias, the seven, the seeds
Of the future) and the heliotrope
Born of your hands – all burned, sucked dry
By a pollen that cries like fire
And is winged with ice and salt.

                              O this ulcered
Spring will still be festival, if it can freeze again
In death that death! Observe once more
Up yonder, Clizia, your destiny, you

Preserved through change by a love which does not change
Until the blind sun you carry in you
Blinds itself in that other, and confounds itself
In Him, for all.

       Perhaps the sirens and the bells
Which salute the monsters in the night
At their witch's sabbath are already confounded
With the sound which unloosed from heaven descends and
   conquers –
With the breath of a dawn which may yet reappear
Tomorrow, white but without wings
Of terror, to the parched arroyos of the south.

            [ME]

The season is Spring, the scene Florence, the day that of the feast of San Giovanni, patron of the city, whose festival is celebrated with fireworks. The moment is that of the visit of the Fuehrer, who rides through the streets accompanied by the Duce and their henchmen. The festival thus becomes a grotesquely unholy holy day, whose real meaning is symbolized by the forced closing of the shops, including toyshops and butcher shops where, following custom, the young goat is crowned with a garland as soon as it is killed. (*Translator's note*)

In the Greenhouse

A pattering of moles
filled up the lemon trees,
in a rosary of cautious drops
the scythe was glittering.

Upon quinces ignited
a point, a lady-bug; the pony
was heard to rear under the curry-comb
– then dreaming overcame.

Ravished, all air, I was permeated
by you, your form became my own
hidden breathing, your
face melted into mine, and the obscure

idea of God descended
upon the few living, among
celestial soundings and infant drummings
and hanging spheres of lightnings,

upon me, and you, and the lemon trees . . .

[JM]

The Shadow of the Magnolia

The shadow of the Japanese magnolia
thins out now that its purple buds
have fallen. At the top intermittently
a cigale vibrates. It is no longer
the time of the choir in unison, Sunflower,
the time of the unlimited godhead
whose faithful it devours that it may feed them.
It was easier to use oneself up, to die
at the first beating of wings, at the first encounter
with the enemy; that was child's play. Henceforth
begins the harder path: but not you, eaten
by sun, and rooted, and withal delicate
thrush soaring high above the cold
wharves of your river – not you, fragile
fugitive to whom zenith nadir cancer
capricorn remains indistinct
because the war was within you and within
whoso adores upon you the wounds of your Spouse,
flinch in the shivering frost . . . The others
retreat and shrivel. The file that subtly
engraves will be silenced, the empty husk
of the singer will soon be powdered
glass underfoot, the shade is livid –
it is autumn, it is winter, it is the beyond
that draws you and into which I throw myself, a mullet's
leap into dryness under the new moon.
Goodbye.

[JM]

The Eel

The eel, the North Sea siren,
who leaves dead-pan Icelandic gods
and the Baltic for our Mediterranean,
our estuaries, our rivers —
who lances through their profound places,
and flinty portages, from branch to branch,
twig to twig, thinning down now,
ever snaking inward, worming
for the granite's heartland, threading
delicate capillaries of slime —
and in the Romagna one morning
the blaze of the chestnut blossoms
ignites its smudge in the dead water
pooled from chiselings
of the Apennines . . .
the eel, a whipstock, a Roman candle,
love's arrow on earth, which only
reaches the paradise of fecundity
through our gullies and fiery, charred streams;
a green spirit, potent only
where desolation and arson burn;
a spark that says everything
begins where everything is clinker;
this buried rainbow, this iris, twin sister
of the one you set in your eye's target center
to shine on the sons of men,
on us, up to our gills in your life-giving mud —
can you call her *Sister*?

[RL]

Little Testament

This that at night keeps flashing
in the calotte of my mind,
mother-of-pearl trace of the snail
or emery of brayed glass,

is neither light of church or factory
that may sustain
clerical red, or black.
Only this iris can I
leave you as testimony
of a faith that was much disputed,
of a hope that burned more slowly
than a hard log in the fireplace.
Conserve its powder in your compact
when every lamplight spent
the sardana becomes infernal
and a shadowy Lucifer descends on a prow
of the Thames or Hudson or Seine
thrashing bituminous wings half-
shorn from the effort, to tell you: it's time.
There's no inheritance, no goodluck charm
that can ward off the monsoons' impact
on the gossamer of memory,
but a history endures in ashes alone
and persistence is only extinction.
Just was the sign: he who has realized it
cannot fail to find you again.
Everyone recognizes his own: pride
was not flight, humility was not
vile, the tenuous glitter polished up
down there was not that of a match.

[CC]

CESARE PAVESE   1908–50

'Death shall come, using your eyes'

Death shall come, using your eyes –
the death that is with us
from morning till night, unsleeping,
muted like old remorse
or some foolish vice. Your eyes
will be an empty word,
a cry suppressed, a silence.
Like this each morning you
see it, when you lean alone
over the mirror. O cherished hope,
that day we too shall know
that you are life and nothingness.

Death has a look for everyone.
Death shall come, using your eyes.
It will be like ending a vice,
like seeing a dead face
emerge from the mirror,
like hearing closed lips speak.
We'll go down in silence.

22 March 1950   [MC]

I shall go through the Piazza di Spagna

The sky will be clear.
The streets will open
below the hills of pine and stone.
No din of the streets will
change this motionless air.
The colour-sprinkled flowers
by the fountains
will look on like women
amused. The steps

the terraces the swallows
will sing in the sun.
That street will open,
the stones will sing,
the heart will beat, leaping
like water in fountains –
this will be the voice
climbing your steps.
The windows will know
the smell of stone and the morning
air. A door will open.
The din of the streets,
the din of the heart,
the light is bewildered.

It will be you – firm and clear.

28 March 1950   [MC]

PRIMO LEVI   1919–87

Shemà

You who live safe
In your warm houses,
You who come home at evening to find
Hot food and friendly faces:

> Consider if this is a man,
> Who toils in the mud
> Who knows no peace
> Who fights for a chunk of bread
> Who dies at a yes or a no.
> Consider if this is a woman,
> Without hair and without name
> Without strength to remember
> Empty eyes and cold womb
> Like a frog in winter.

Be mindful that this has been:
I urge these words on you.
Carve them on your heart
At home or roaming the streets
Lying down or rising up:
Repeat them to your children.
Or may your house fall,
Sickness lay you low,
Your offspring turn their faces from you.

10 January 1946   [AA]

Reveille

In the brutal nights we used to dream
Dense violent dreams,
Dreamed with soul and body:
To return; to eat; to tell the story.
Until the dawn command

Sounded brief, low:
  '*Wstawać*':
And the heart cracked in the breast.

Now we have found our homes again,
Our bellies are full,
We're through telling the story.
It's time. Soon we'll hear again
The strange command:
  '*Wstawać*'.

11 January 1946   [RF/BS]

Wstawać means 'Get up!' in Polish. (*Translator's note*)

The Gulls of Settimo

From meander to meander, year by year,
The lords of the sky have come up the river,
Along the banks, up from its violent mouths.
They have forgotten surf and salt water,
The crafty patient hunts, voracious crabs.
Up through Crespino, Polesella, Ostiglia,
The newborn more determined than the old,
Beyond Luzzara, beyond dead Viadana,
Greedy for our ignoble refuse,
Fatter from bend to bend.
They have explored Caorso's mists,
The lazy branches between Cremona and Piacenza.
Borne on the superhighway's tepid breath,
Mournfully shrieking their brief greeting,
They have paused at the Ticino's mouth,
Built nests under Valenza's bridge
Among tar-clots and polyethylene scraps.
They've sailed to the mountain, beyond Casale and Chivasso,
Fleeing the sea and lured by our abundance.
Now they hover restlessly above Settimo Torinese,
And, forgetful of the past, ransack our rubbish.

9 April 1979   [RF]

The Survivor

To B.V.

> *Dopo di allora, ad ora incerta,*
> Since then, at an uncertain hour,
> That agony returns:
> And till my ghastly tale is told,
> This heart within me burns.

Once more he sees his companions' faces
Livid in the first faint light,
Gray with cement dust,
Nebulous in the mist,
Tinged with death in their uneasy sleep.
At night, under the heavy burden
Of their dreams, their jaws move,
Chewing a nonexistent turnip.
'Stand back, leave me alone, submerged people,
Go away. I haven't dispossessed anyone,
Haven't usurped anyone's bread.
No one died in my place. No one.
Go back into your mist.
It's not my fault if I live and breathe,
Eat, drink, sleep and put on clothes.'

4 February 1984   [RF]

The Elephant

Dig and you'll find my bones,
Absurd in this snow-filled place.
I was tired of marching and heavy loads;
I missed the warmth and grass.
You'll find coins and Punic weapons
Buried by avalanches: absurd, absurd!
Absurd my story and that of History.
What were Carthage and Rome to me?
Now my fine ivory, our pride and joy,
Noble, curved like the crescent moon,
Lies splintered among the river's stones.

It wasn't made for piercing breastplates
But for digging up roots and pleasing females.
We fight only for mates,
Wisely, without bloodshed.
Would you like to hear my story? It's brief.
The cunning Indian trapped and tamed me,
The Egyptian shackled and sold me,
The Phoenician covered me with armour
And set a tower on my back.
It was absurd that I, a tower of flesh,
Invulnerable, gentle and terrible,
Forced here among these enemy mountains,
Slipped on your ice I'd never seen before.
When one of us falls down, there is no saving him.
A bold blind man tried for a long time
To find my heart with his lance-point.
I've hurled my useless dying trumpeting
At these peaks,
Livid in the sunset: 'Absurd, absurd.'

23 March 1984   [RF]

The 'bold blind man' is Hannibal who, according to tradition, contracted an
eye disease while crossing the Alps. (*Translator's note*)

Sidereus Nuncius

I have seen two-horned Venus
Travelling gently in the sky.
I have seen valleys and mountains on the Moon,
Saturn with its three bodies;
I, Galileo, first among humans,
Have seen four stars circle round Jupiter,
The Milky Way split into
Countless legions of new worlds.
I have seen, unbelieved, ominous spots
Foul the Sun's face.
This spyglass was made by me,
A man of learning but with clever hands;

I've polished its lenses, aimed it at the Heavens
As you would aim a bombard.
I am the one who broke open the Sky
Before the Sun burned my eyes.
    Before the Sun burned my eyes
    I had to stoop to saying
    I did not see what I saw.
    The one who bound me to the earth
    Did not unleash earthquakes or lightning.
    His voice was subdued and smooth;
    He had the face of everyman.
    The vulture that gnaws me every evening
    Has everyman's face.

11 April 1984   [RF]

Galileo saw three bodies of Saturn because of imperfections in his spyglass.
(*Translator's note*)

The Opus

There, it's finished: leave it alone.
How heavy my pen feels in my hand!
It was so light just a moment ago,
Alive, like quicksilver:
I had only to follow it.
It led my hand
Like a dog leads a blind man,
Like a lady leads you to a dance.
Now it's over, the work is finished,
Perfected, rounded.
If I were to take a single word away
There would be a hole oozing pus.
If I were to add one
It would stick out like an ugly boil.

If I were to change one, it would be out of tune,
Like a dog howling at a concert.
What to do now? How to detach yourself?
For every work that's born you die a little.

[AA/GS]

FRANCE

FRANCIS PONGE   1899–1988

The Wasp-woman

I

She could only mate in the air. Her body,
    a little heavier than
a mosquito's, the wings light and small, beating,

hovered in a million cells. Each spent moment
    she seemed to quiver as if
pinned on a fly-paper or drowning in thick

honey. She moved as if trapped always at a
    point of crisis which made her
the danger she was. Like a taut string whose touch

burned or cut as it yielded its resonance,
    she hurt as she moved. From her
belly the rich beating came. On the skin of

plums her nails moved like a machine for plucking
    something out. If her clothes rasped
on the edge of a plate, or brushed a cup where

the dregs of sugar remained, you could feel the
    dark pull of the world's honey,
straining her muscles.

II

                The electric tram moves

on its rails. There is something deaf in repose
    and loud into gear about
it too. It breaks at the waist as she did. Is

shrivelled by electricity like something
    fried. And if you touched her, she
pricked. No shock, the venomous vibration from

all her pores: but her body was softer, her
    flight wilder, more unforeseen,
more dangerous than the even run of a

thing on rails.

III

                         She was one of those wheeled machines
    that at certain seasons ride
from farm to farm in the country, providing

refreshment. A little pump grinding on wings.
    Nobody knowing how she
maintained her internal state of a tense poise

or constructed what she was selling. Whose whole
    activity was inside,
a thing of mystery and presumed wisdom.

A cauldron of jam, sealed from the air, and yet
    soft. And the drum in the groin
causing her to see-saw, as she rose in flight.

IV

One must always classify what is known by
    a character which endures,
and by which one could recognize it. And so

with her it is that skin. Perhaps rightly. I
    know nothing of it, I could
never swear to it. And yet with that wasp it

was not so odd to describe her wings as *like*
    membranes. Not that they looked like
a dark hymen. It was for historical

reasons. The abstraction remains, trailing the
    hard truths of a thing once felt.
In the coils of the living science there lies

the stretched, gauzy, tendentious, appropriate
    words for a wasp-woman. There
is nothing more in this line.

V

What else can one

say? That she left her sting in the victim and
          succumbs to it? In war that
never pays. The elaborate touchiness —

from fear or from over-sensitivity —
          has already punished her.
She has no advantage in risking a new

enemy, would zig-zag to miss a friend. *I
          know my ways*, she would say, *if
I attach myself it can only provoke*

*a crisis. We are too far apart. If once
          I accepted the pulse of
your world, I should spend my life in it. So launch*

*me in my groove and go on in yours. In the
          sleep-walking, the internal
deadness. Forget about explaining things.* It

was then that the world gave her a little knock,
          and she dropped. I could only
crush her to death.

VI

(Or was it perhaps that she

was touchy because of what she carried? And
          this justified her rage: her
consciousness of its value?)

VII

And yet this fine

deadness which could destroy her (one blow, and she
          dropped) could also save her, or
at least prolong her life. That dark wasp was so

stupid (I don't mean to abuse her) that if
          you cut her in two parts, she
continued to live. She took two days to know

she was dead. Her heart just went on beating. It
    beat faster than before. And
surely this was the zenith of preventive

stupidity? Stupidity in the gut.

   VIII
    Swarm: from exagmen: from *ex*
agire: to push out.

   IX
                       Such thirst perhaps from

the slenderness of her waist. For the Greeks the
    brain was in the waist. And they
used the same word for both. If it was *sponge*, they

were right.

   X
                  Why was it so? That of all creatures
    the fiercest one was the sun's
colour? And why are beaten things always the

savagest?

   XI
                 She thrust into flesh as others
    delve into fruit. Would wrestle,
mouth, warp, corrupt it. With her elastic-smooth,

marmalade-black body would smash, pulp, erase
    the integrity of flesh,
even alter its feel of being alive.

When a wasp bites at a fruit there is never
    such love-loathing, such many-
legged, insectuous writhing. She worked like a

black chemical, a violent process of
    decomposition, marring
the flesh to a mess of pulp, exhausting the

seed.

XII
                         Listen to the plum speaking. *When the sun
     ejaculates his honey,*
it scorches my skin. If the brisk wasp works her

sting into me, it rips my guts.

XIII
                                             And she was
     always eager for the full
honey-bin. Her temples quivering, her skin

trembling, and then the butterflies in her crutch:
     a sort of squirt for sucking
sweetness in.

XIV
                         First there was the furnace. And then

the half-charred wasp was born, hissing, terrible
     and by no means a matter
of indifference to Men-kind, for they faced

in her burning elegance their abortive
     hunger for speed and for closed
flight through air. And in mine I saw an earthed fire

whose wings gushed out in all directions, and on
     unforeseen trajectories.
It burned as if on offensive missions from

a nest in the ground. Like an engine out of
     control, sometimes it trembled
as though she were not the mistress of her own

destructiveness. So at first that fire spread in
     the earth, crackling, fluttering:
and then when the wings were accomplished, the sexed

wings, the antennaed squadrons broke out on their
     deadly business into the
flesh, and their work began to be finished, I

mean, her crime.

XV

In her swarm of words, the abrupt
    waspishness. But wait. Was this
devised flutter in the trench any more than

the weak rebellion of a few seeds, outraged
    by their sower? It was their
own violence that first brought them into his

apron. No, go back. This was a fire whose wings
    gushed out in all directions,
and on unforeseen trajectories. And I

faced in her burned elegance my abortive
    hunger for speed and for closed
flight through air. Or must one look further. Here was

the natural world on the wing. Her cruel
    divisions preparing their
offensive against male tyranny. I bared

my forests for their sting. But already her
    banked animosity was
flowing away in random fury . . .

XVI

A swarm

of mute wasps worked over the countryside: and
    my unprotected nerves were
worked over by her.

XVII

And then one knock, one sharp

gun-shot. And she seemed (herself like a gun-shot
    recovering her fallen
decisiveness) to hurl herself with all haste

on her certain death. No, not quite. Like a shot,
    but less direct. As if when
the bullets left the gun the air seduced them

into forgetting their first intention, their
    straight road, their bitterness. Or
as if an army were sent to occupy

the nerve centres of a key city, and, once
    inside the main gates, became
absorbed into the bright things in windows, and

visited the museums, and drank from the
    straws of the men sipping wine
at the sidewalk cafés.

   XVIII
                        And like gun-shots the

little nibbling bits she had once taken out
    of a thing saved up: as a
wasp riddles an upright wall of wormeaten

wood.

   XIX
               Or you could call her the instrument of
    that world-honey I spoke of
earlier. I mean a pent sweetness, needling,

repeated, beginning feebly, but awkward
    to shake off, and then striking
clear, with alternating force and weakness, and

so on. As the crisp wasp might well be called the
    musical form of honey:
ringing, insistent, devouring and fragile.

   XX
And so on. Perhaps one day there will be a
    critic. And he will REPROACH
me for so inserting into poetry

my importunate, irritating and dead
    wasp-woman. And will DENOUNCE
the seductive appeal of her, and the way

she appears in so many sharp pieces, and
    zig-zags. And will be DISTURBED
at her lack of smooth co-ordination, and

piquancy without depth (though not without some
    danger) and all that. And will
treat my wasp-woman with all the abuse and

puzzlement she so richly deserves. I shall
    not worry, dear reader. The
harm was first done by a French poet in prose.

[GM]

PHILIPPE JACCOTTET   1925–

Ignorance

The older I grow the more ignorant I become,
the longer I live the less I possess or control.
All I have is a little space, snow-dark
or glittering, never inhabited.
Where is the giver, the guide, the guardian?
I sit in my room and am silent. Silence
arrives like a servant to tidy things up
while I wait for the lies to disperse.
And what remains to this dying man
that so well prevents him from dying?
What does he find to say to the four walls?
I hear him talking still, and his words
come in with the dawn, imperfectly understood:

'Love, like fire, can only reveal its brightness
on the failure and the beauty of burnt wood.'

[DM]

Distances

Swifts turn in the heights of the air;
higher still turn the invisible stars.
When day withdraws to the ends of the earth
their fires shine on a dark expanse of sand.

We live in a world of motion and distance.
The heart flies from tree to bird,
from bird to distant star,
from star to love; and love grows
in the quiet house, turning and working,
servant of thought, a lamp held in one hand.

[DM]

End of Winter

Not much, nothing to dispel
the fear of wasting space
is left the itinerant soul

Except perhaps a voice
unconfident and light,
uncertainly put forth,
with which to celebrate
the reaches of the earth

[DM]

'Each flower is a little night'

Each flower is a little night
pretending to draw near

But where its scent rises
I cannot hope to enter
which is why it bothers me
so much and why I sit so long
before this closed door

Each colour, each incarnation
begins where the eyes stop

This world is merely the tip
of an unseen conflagration

[DM]

'Grapes and figs'

Grapes and figs
born far off in the mountains
under the slow clouds
and the fresh air –
oh yes, oh yes . . .

But there comes a time
when the eldest, tired,
retires early; from day to day
his step grows less assured.

No longer a question
of moving about
like water between its banks;
and this won't improve.

When the master himself
is taken so far so quickly
I look for what may follow –

not a lamp of fruit,
a fearless bird,
the purest of images,

but water and clean linen,
the loving hand
and the obstinate heart.

[DM]

'Who will help me? No one can come this far'

'Who will help me? No one can come this far.
Holding my hands won't stop them shaking,
shading my eyes won't stop them seeing,
being close to me day and night like a coat
can do nothing against this heat, this cold.
I can at least confirm there is a wall here
that no invading force will ever destroy.
There's nothing for it now but the longest and worst.'

Is this what he whispers to the narrowing night?

[DM]

'It's easy to talk'

It's easy to talk, and writing words on the page
doesn't involve much risk as a general rule:
you might as well be knitting late at night
in a warm room, in a soft, treacherous light.
The words are all written in the same ink,
'flower' and 'fear' are nearly the same for example,
and I could scrawl 'blood' the length of the page
without splashing the paper or hurting
myself at all.

After a while it gets you down, this game,
you no longer know what it was you set out to achieve
instead of exposing yourself to life
and doing something useful with your hands.

That's when you can't escape,
when pain is a figure tearing the fog
that shrouds you, striking away
the obstacles one by one, covering
the swiftly decreasing distance, now
so close you can make out nothing
but his mug wider than the sky.

To speak is to lie, or worse: a craven
insult to grief or a waste
of the little time and energy at our disposal.

[DM]

'Quick write this book'

Quick write this book, quick finish this poem today
before self-doubt can hinder you,
before the distracting cloud
of questions leads you astray.

Finish the line, fill up the page before
the trembling starts, the trembling born
of illness, fear, distraction,

before thin air replaces the blue wall
you're leaning against. Sometimes already
the bell goes wrong in the bone belfry,
banging fit to split the stones.

Don't write 'for the angel in the church of the Laodiceans'
but without knowing for whom, on the air,
with uncertain, tentative bat-signs.
Quick, clear this space again with your hand;
bind, weave, clothe us shivering beasts,
us baffled moles, cover us up
with a last strip of golden light
as the sun covers the poplars and the mountains.

[DM]

'I rise with an effort and look out'

I rise with an effort and look out
at three different kinds of light –
that of the sky, that which from up there
pours into me and vanishes,
and that whose shadow my hand draws on the page.

The ink might be mistaken for shadow.

The sky descending takes me by surprise.

One would like to believe we suffer
to describe the light from above;
but pain is stronger than flight
and pity drowns everything, shining
with as many tears as the night.

[DM]

Glimpses

The children run shouting
in the thick grass of the playground.

The tall tranquil trees
and the torrential light
of a September morning
protect them still from the anvil
sparkling with stars up there.

*

The soul, so chilly, so fierce, must it really
trudge up this glacier for ever,
solitary, in bare feet, no longer
remembering even its childhood prayer,
its coldness for ever punished by this cold?

*

Wrapped in a blue bath-robe
which is wearing out too,
she goes to a mirror round
like the mouth of a child
who doesn't know how to lie.

Hair the colour of ash now
in the slow burn of time;

and yet the morning sun
quickens her shadow still.

*

At the window with its freshly whitewashed frame
(to keep out flies, to keep out ghosts)
the white head of an old man leans
over a letter or the local news.
Against the wall dark ivy grows.

Save him, ivy and lime, from the dawn wind,
from long nights and the other, eternal night.

[DM]

To Henry Purcell

Listen: how is it
that our troubled voice mingles like this
with the stars?

He has scaled the heavens
on rungs of glass
by the youthful grace of his art.

　*

We hear the passing of ewes
who throng the dust of the celestial summer,
whose milk we have never drunk.

He has herded them into the fold of night
where straw shines among the stones,
and the gate bangs shut.
The coolness of these quiet grasses for ever . . .

　*

What do we hear
who tune in to the night?
A leisurely snow
of crystal.

　*

Imagine a comet
returning centuries hence
from the kingdom of the dead,
crossing our century tonight
and sowing the same seeds . . .

　*

While I listen
the reflection of a candle
flickers in the mirror
like a flame woven
of water.

Might not this voice be the echo
of another, more real?
and will that ever be heard
by those thrashing in terror?
Will I hear it myself?

If ever they speak above us
in the starry trees of their April.

*

You are seated before
the tense loom of the harp.

I know you, though invisible,
weaver of supernatural streams.

[DM]

AUSTRIA

ERICH FRIED   1921–88

Transformation

My girl-friends turn slowly
over three or four weeks
or quickly over night
into my aunts and old cousins

I see them chew anxiously
at their dentures
and with gouty fingers dry
the spittle from their faces

With cases and bundles
they arrive in Theresienstadt
They fumble for their glasses
as they fall from the window

Curled up in bed
they try to come to attention
so as to be spared
when they weed out the sick

When I kiss them in the morning
I see their bluish tint
piled six high
washed clean with garden-hoses

of shit and vomited slime
ready for transport
from the gas-chamber
to the cremation oven
                    [SH]

Theresienstadt or Teresin was a concentration camp, mainly for old people.
(*Translator's note*)

Conservation of Matter

Every morning
I am embalmed

the mouth is rinsed out
with bitter essences

the dreams are forgotten
the hair combed

the teeth cleaned
the eyes opened wider

In the mirror before shaving
a deep breath is taken

after shaving
the skin of the face is rejuvenated

with spirit
and the hair with an atomiser

courage is taken
something warm gets into the stomach

Then I disintegrate
towards the next morning

[SH]

Death Certificate

'Because it's all no use
They do as they please anyhow

Because I don't want to get
my fingers burnt again

Because they'll just laugh:
it only needed you!

And why always me?
I'll get no thanks for it

Because no one can sort this out
One might only make things worse

Because even what's bad
may have some good in it

Because it depends how you look at it
and anyway whom can you trust?

Because the other side too
gets wet when it rains

Because I'd rather leave it
to those more qualified

Because you never know
what you let yourself in for

Because it's a waste of effort
They don't deserve it'

These are the causes of death
to write on our graves

which will not even be dug
if these are the causes

                     [GR]

What Happens

It has happened
and it goes on happening
and will happen again
if nothing happens to stop it

The innocent know nothing
because they are too innocent
and the guilty know nothing
because they are too guilty

The poor do not notice
because they are too poor

and the rich do not notice
because they are too rich

The stupid shrug their shoulders
because they are too stupid
and the clever shrug their shoulders
because they are too clever

The young do not care
because they are too young
and the old do not care
because they are too old

That is why nothing happens
to stop it
and that is why it has happened
and goes on happening and will happen again

                                                                      [SH]

Premonition of Final Victory

Sisyphus
dusty
and full
of the fine flour
of his stone
is afraid
The stone is wearing away

The senselessness
the eternally accursed
sense of his labour
is itself
struck by the curse

Smaller
like the dwindling stone
the mercy of the shades
that give him
the strength to be helpless

Soon only a pebble
will roll
on the flayed slope
What remains?

Nothing but the torture
of having outlived
his torture

    [SH]

Old Salts

In the ears the sounds of distant coasts
are only shouts in a harbour
the rattle of anchor-chains
rumbling of trains
revving of heavy lorries
the screams of beaten women
and the belling
of ships' sirens
at the rutting-time of the navies of Christendom

In their noses the smell of strange lands
is sweat and dust
and half-stale spices
and children's urine in dank quarters
and rot-gut
and city dust after summer rain
and hot walls in the evening
and paint and grease
and cheap whore's perfume

And what they think are the colours of cities
making eyes at them
is only the blind colour
of their poverty in every city
And their boasting
about their long journeys
only means:

We have got about a lot
in our misery

[SH]

The Measures Taken

The lazy are slaughtered
the world grows industrious

The ugly are slaughtered
the world grows beautiful

The foolish are slaughtered
the world grows wise

The sick are slaughtered
the world grows healthy

The sad are slaughtered
the world grows merry

The old are slaughtered
the world grows young

The enemies are slaughtered
the world grows friendly

The wicked are slaughtered
the world grows good

1958   [MH]

Unoccupied Room

The dust in this room
delicate on the windowpanes
the quiet dust
on the table
on the old cushion:
peach skin down
that fondles the fondling hand

that shows the sun
the way through fastened windows

To be tired
and unwilling to weep
and unwilling
to die
to have wept and to be already dead:
In the light dust
that shows sunlight the way
to lie on the cushion
not again
but always
and still
and already for always
dust on dust amid dust

Dust on the table
on the bed
on the windowpanes:
dust in dust
sun in dust
dust in the sun
I dust in the room of the sun
I dust on the cushion
I Again I Still I Always
in the room of dust

1959–67   [MH]

INGEBORG BACHMANN   1926–73

To the Sun

More beautiful than the remarkable moon and her noble light,
More beautiful than the stars, the famous medals of night,
Much more beautiful than the fiery entrance a comet makes,
And called to a part far more splendid than any other planet's
Because daily your life and my life depend on it, is the sun.

Beautiful sun that rises, his work not forgotten,
And completes it, most beautifully in summer, when a day
Evaporates on the coast, and effortlessly mirrored the sails
Pass through your sight, till you tire and cut short the last.

Without the sun even art takes the veil again,
You cease to appear to me, and the sea and the sand,
Lashed by shadows, take refuge under my eyelids.

Beautiful light, that keeps us warm, preserves us, marvellously
    makes sure
That I see again and that I see you again!

Nothing more beautiful under the sun than to be under the sun . . .

Nothing more beautiful than to see the stick in water and the bird
    above,
Pondering his flight, and, below, the fishes in shoals,

Coloured, moulded, brought into the world with a mission of light,
And to see the radius, the square of a field, my landscape's thousand
    angles

And the dress you have put on. And *your* dress, bell-shaped and
    blue!
Beautiful blue, in which peacocks walk and bow.
Blue of far places, the zones of joy with weathers that suit my mood,
Blue chance on the horizon! And my enchanted eyes
Dilate again and blink and burn themselves sore.

Beautiful sun, to whom dust owes great admiration yet,
Not for the moon, therefore, and not for the stars, and not

Because night shows off with comets, trying to fool me,
But for your sake, and endlessly soon, and for you above all
I shall lament the inevitable loss of my sight.

1956   [MH]

Fog Land

In winter my loved one retires
to live with the beasts of the forest.
That I must be back before morning
the vixen knows well, and she laughs.
Now the low clouds quiver! And down
on my upturned collar there falls
a landslide of brittle ice.

In winter my loved one retires,
a tree among trees, and invites
the crows in their desolation
into her beautiful boughs. She knows
that as soon as night falls the wind
lifts her stiff, hoar-frost-embroidered
evening gown, sends me home.

In winter my loved one retires,
a fish among fishes, and dumb.
Slave to the waters she ripples
with her fins' gentle motion within,
I stand on the bank and look down
till ice floes drive me away,
her dipping and turning hidden.

And stricken again by the blood-cry
of the bird that tautens his wings
over my head, I fall down
on the open field: she is plucking
the hens, and she throws me a whitened
collar bone. This round my neck,
off I go through the bitter down.

My loved one, I know, is unfaithful,
and sometimes she stalks and she hovers
on high-heeled shoes to the city
and deeply in bars with her straw
will kiss the lips of the glasses,
and finds words for each and for all.
But this language is alien to me.

It is fog land I have seen.
It is fog heart I have eaten.

1956   [MH]

Every Day

War is no longer declared
but continued. The unheard-of thing
is the everyday. The hero
keeps away from the fighters. The weak man
has moved up to the battle zones.
The uniform of the day is patience,
its decoration the humble star
of hope worn over the heart.

It is awarded
when nothing goes on,
when the barrage subsides,
when the enemy has grown invisible
and the shadow of everlasting arms
covers the sky.

It is awarded
for desertion of the flag,
for courage in the face of the friend,
for the betrayal of unworthy secrets
and for the nonobservance
of every order.

1957   [MH]

The Respite

A harder time is coming.
The end of the respite allowed us
appears on the skyline.
Soon you must tie your shoelace
and drive back the dogs to the marshland farms.
For the fishes' entrails
have grown cold in the wind.
Poorly the light of the lupins burns.
Your gaze gropes in the fog:
the end of the respite allowed us
appears on the skyline.

Over there your loved one sinks in the sand,
it rises towards her blown hair,
it cuts short her speaking,
it commands her to be silent,
it finds that she is mortal
and willing to part
after every embrace.

Do not look round.
Tie your shoelace.
Drive back the dogs.
Throw the fishes into the sea.
Put out the lupins!

A harder time is coming.

1957   [MH]

Exile

A dead man I am who travels
not registered anywhere
unknown in the realm of prefects
redundant in the golden cities
and in the countryside's green

written off long ago
and provided with nothing

Only with wind with time and with sound

who cannot live among human beings

I with the German language
this cloud around me
that I keep as a house
drive through all languages

Oh, how it darkens
those muted those rain tones
only few of them fall

Up into brighter zones it will carry the dead man

1964   [MH]

GREECE

YANNIS RITSOS

1909–91

Morning

She opened the shutters. She hung the sheets over the sill. She saw the
    day.
A bird looked at her straight in the eyes. 'I am alone,' she whispered.
'I am alive.' She entered the room. The mirror too is a window.
If I jump from it I will fall into my arms.

[NS]

Almost a Conjurer

From a distance he lowers the light of the oil lamp, he moves the
    chairs
without touching them. He gets tired. He takes off his hat and fans
    himself.
Then, with a drawn-out gesture, he produces three playing cards
from the side of his ear. He dissolves a green, pain-soothing star
in a glass of water, stirring it with a silver spoon.
He drinks the water and the spoon. He becomes transparent.
A goldfish can be seen swimming inside his chest.
Then, exhausted, he leans on the sofa and shuts his eyes.
'I have a bird in my head,' he says. 'I can't get it out.'
The shadows of two huge wings fill the room.

[NS]

The Suspect

He locked the door. He looked suspiciously behind him
and shoved the key in his pocket. It was just then he was arrested.
They tortured him for months. Until, one evening, he confessed
(which was considered proof) that the key and the house
were his own. But no one understood

why he should try to hide the key. And so,
despite his acquittal, he remained to them a suspect.

[NS]

Approximately

He picks up in his hands things that don't match – a stone,
a broken roof-tile, two burned matches,
the rusty nail from the wall opposite,
the leaf that came in through the window, the drops
dropping from the watered flower pots, that bit of straw
the wind blew in your hair yesterday – he takes them
and he builds, in his backyard, approximately a tree.
Poetry is in this 'approximately'. Can you see it?

[NS]

Submission

She opened the window. The wind struck,
with a burst, her hair, like two big birds,
over her shoulders. She shut the window.
The two birds were on the table
looking at her. She lowered her head
between them and cried quietly.

[NS]

First Pleasure

Proud mountains, Kallidromon, Oite, Othrys,
sovereign rocks, vines, wheat and olive groves;
They've made quarries here, the sea has pulled back;
strong smell of sun-burnt mastic trees,
the resin dripping in clots. Big
descending night. There, on the bank, Achilles,
not yet an adolescent, as he was tying his sandals,
felt that special pleasure as he held

his heel in his palm. His mind wandered for a moment
as he looked at the reflections in the water. Then
he went into the smithy to order his shield –
he knew now the shape in every detail, the scenes depicted on it, the
    size.

[NS]

The Potter

One day he finished with the pitchers, the flower pots, the cooking
    pots. Some clay
was left over. He made a woman. Her breasts
were big and firm. His mind wandered. He returned home late.
His wife grumbled. He didn't answer her. Next day
he kept more clay and even more the following day.
He wouldn't go back home. His wife left him.
His eyes burn. He's half-naked. He wears a red waist-band.
He lies all night with clay women. At dawn
you can hear him sing behind the fence of the workshop.
He took off his red waist-band too. Naked. Completely naked.
    And all around him
the empty pitchers, the empty cooking pots, the empty flower pots
and the beautiful, blind, deaf-and-dumb women with the bitten
    breasts.

[NS]

After the Defeat

After the destruction of the Athenians at the Aegospotami, a little
    later,
after our final defeat, free discussions, the Periclean glory,
the flourishing of the arts, the gymnasiums, the symposia of our
    philosophers have all vanished. Now
gloom, a heavy silence in the marketplace, and the impurity of the
    Thirty Tyrants.
Everything (even what is most our own) happens by default without
chance for appeal, defence or justification,

or even formal protest. Our papers and our books are burned,
the honour of our country rots. Even if an old friend could be
      allowed
to come as witness, he would refuse out of fear
of getting in the same trouble – he would be right, of course. So,
it is better to be here – who knows, maybe we can acquire a fresh
      contact with nature,
looking at a fragment of the sea, the stones, the weeds,
or at a cloud at sunset, deep, violet, moving, behind the barbed wire.
      And maybe
a new Kimon will arrive one day, secretly led
by the same eagle, and he'll dig and find our iron spear point,
rusty, that too almost disintegrated, and he might go
to Athens and carry it in a procession of mourning or triumph with
      music and with wreaths.

                              [NS]

Penelope's Despair

Not that she didn't recognize him in the dim light of the fire,
his disguise in beggar's rags. No. There were clear signs:
the scar on the knee-cap, his muscular body, the cunning look.
      Frightened,
leaning against the wall, she tried to find some excuse, a delay to
      avoid answering
so as not to betray her thoughts. Was it for him she had wasted
      twenty years
waiting and dreaming? Was it for this wretched stranger
soaked in blood, with his white beard? She fell speechless on a chair,
she looked closely at the slaughtered suitors on the floor as if looking
at her own dead desires and she said 'welcome',
her voice sounding to her as if it came from a distance, as if someone
      else's. The loom in the corner
cast shadows across the ceiling like a cage, the birds she had woven
with bright red threads among green leaves suddenly
turned grey and black
flying low on the flat sky of her final endurance.

                              [NS]

Search

Come in, Gentlemen – he said. No inconvenience. Look through
    everything;
I have nothing to hide. Here's the bedroom, here the study,
here the dining-room. Here? – the attic for old things; –
everything wears out, Gentlemen; it's full; everything wears out,
    wears out,
so quickly too, Gentlemen; this? – a thimble; – mother's;
this? mother's oil-lamp, mother's umbrella – she loved me enor-
    mously; –
but this forged identity card? this jewellery, somebody else's? the
    dirty towel?
this theatre ticket? the shirt with holes? blood stains?
and this photograph? his, yes, wearing a woman's hat covered with
    flowers,
inscribed to a stranger – his handwriting –
who planted these in here? who planted these in here? who planted
    these in here?

                                                            [NS]

ROMANIA

Destiny

The chicken I bought last night,
Frozen,
Returned to life,
Laid the biggest egg in the world,
And was awarded the Nobel Prize.

The phenomenal egg
Was passed from hand to hand,
In a few weeks had gone all round the earth,
And round the sun
In 365 days.

The hen received who knows how much hard currency,
Assessed in buckets of grain
Which she couldn't manage to eat

Because she was invited everywhere,
Gave lectures, granted interviews,
Was photographed.

Very often the reporters insisted
That I too should pose
Beside her.
And so, having served art
Throughout my life,
All of a sudden I've attained to fame
As a poultry breeder.

[DJE/IRG]

Precautions

I pulled on a suit of mail
made of pebbles
worn smooth by water.

I balanced a pair of glasses
on my neck
so as to keep an eye
on whatever
was coming behind me.

I gloved and greaved
my hands, my legs, my thoughts,
leaving no part of my person
exposed to touch
or other poisons.

Then I fashioned a breastplate
from the shell
of an eight-hundred-year-old
turtle.

And when everything was just so
I tenderly replied:
– I love you too.

    [PM/IRG]

Cure

When the cure for a disease is discovered
Those who have died of the illness
Ought to rise again
And go on living
All the rest of their days
Until they fall sick with another disease
Whose cure has not yet been discovered.

    [DJE/IRG]

Sealess

Visibly, daily,
He was shrinking. The matter of him
Was taking its leave with polite excuses

Stepping back for the running jump
Into another mode.

And the sea too
The sea the poor codger was fishing in
The sea was pulling out.
Oh such an ebb!
One day he was stranded on the mere sand.

She has gone with her waves and fishes
Who knows where and moves now
To and fro, to and fro
Under some younger boat.

[DC/IRG]

Adam

Although he was in Paradise,
Adam walked the paths preoccupied and sad,
Not knowing what he was missing.

Then God fashioned Eve
From one of Adam's ribs.
And the first man liked this miracle so much
That right away
He touched the adjacent rib,
Sensing a delicate tingling in his fingers
From firm breasts and sweet hips
Like the contours of music.
A new Eve had risen in front of him.
She had taken her little mirror out
And was painting her mouth.
'That's life!' sighed Adam,
And created another one.

And thus, whenever the official Eve
Turned her back,
Or went to the market for gold and incense and myrrh,
Adam brought an extra odalisque to life
From his intercostal harem.

God had observed
This disorderly creativity of Adam's.
He summoned him, denounced him divinely,
And expelled him from Paradise
For surrealism.

   [DJE/IRG]

The Compass

The sea is an enormous compass
With nervy fishes
Pointing all the time due north.

Each fish of course holds to
His own north
Which he tries to superimpose
On inferior norths,
Gulping them down while Neptune isn't looking.

Rumour has it that the time will come
For a unique north, scientifically worked out,
When all the fish
Will swim with the tide
Nose to tail
Formation-swimming northwards on their bellies,
Then southwards on their backs.

No longer will ships get lost
At sea
Or be sucked in by whirlpools,
And with such a high-tech compass
The world will, on the whole, have a clearer idea
Of where it stands from day to day.

        [ML/IRG]

The Tear

I weep and weep a tear
Which will not fall
No matter how much I weep.

Its pang in me
Is like the birth of an icicle.

Colder and colder, the earth
Curves on my eyelid,
The northern ice-cap keeps rising.

O, my arctic eyelid.

[SH/IRG]

Evolution

It is time to learn from the bats
The between-creatures
Who can home in the dark.

Learn flying blind.
Dispense with the sun.
The future is dark.

[DC/IRG]

Fountains in the Sea

Water: no matter how much, there is still not enough.
Cunning life keeps asking for more and then a drop more.
Our ankles are weighted with lead, we delve under the wave.
We bend to our spades, we survive the force of the gusher.

Our bodies fountain with sweat in the deep of the sea,
Our forehead aches and holds like a sunken prow.
We are out of breath, divining the heart of the geyser,
Constellations are bobbing like corks above on the swell.

Earth is a waterwheel, the buckets go up and go down,
But to keep the whole aqueous architecture standing its ground
We must make a ring with our bodies and dance out a round
On the dreamt eye of water, the dreamt eye of water, the dreamt eye
    of water.

Water: no matter how much, there is still not enough.
Come rain, come thunder, come deluged dams washed away,
Our thirst is unquenchable. A cloud in the water's a siren.
We become two shades, deliquescent, drowning in song.

My love, under the tall sky of hope
Our love and our love alone
Keeps dowsing for water.
Sinking the well of each other, digging together.
Each one the other's phantom limb in the sea.

[SH/IRG]

Leda

Smiling, Leda mixes
in with things
and sleeps with
everyone.

To the fence in the yard she gives
an ivy baby,
to the sun thing up there
a sunflower.

Shamelessly she did it
with all the oxen,
beginning with Apis,
but, damn it, to look at her
no one would have guessed.

A fine little piece,
that Leda.

Which is why the world
still remains so lovely.

[MH]

The Complaint

They have murdered my time,
Your Honour.

When of my own free will
I returned from the war
I realized
that my time,
heart, mouth and forehead
had been amputated.

But they still wouldn't leave it alone,
it had to absolve days of torment,
days of tears, days of machines, days of oxen
and many other things
it did not care for.

After that they began
to use it for testing
a number of poisons,
griefs and cares –
that's what they called them.

They finished me off
with a well-aimed
blow of fate.

With all due respect,
that wasn't a life.
Meanwhile, in order
to voice my complaint,
I have wasted half my death
standing in queues

here,
at the Last Judgement.

[MH]

The Actors

How strangely limber these actors are!
How good they are
at living for us with their shirtsleeves rolled up!

Never have I seen a more perfect kiss
than theirs in the third act
when their feelings
are being made clear.

Spotty, smeared with oil,
with caps true to life,
performing all sorts of functions,
they come and go as they're prompted
by words that roll out like red carpets.

Their deaths on the boards are so natural
that the real, the
once and for all tragically
made-up dead of the graveyards
seem to stir
at such perfection.

And how much more we, who woodenly
are stuck in a single life!
And are not competent to live that one even.
We who talk nonsense or keep silent for centuries,
awkward and unaesthetic,
not knowing what to do with our hands.

[MH]

RUSSIA

BORIS PASTERNAK   1890–1960

Hamlet

The buzz subsides. I have come on stage.
Leaning in an open door
I try to detect from the echo
What the future has in store.

A thousand opera-glasses level
The dark, point-blank, at me.
Abba, Father, if it be possible
Let this cup pass from me.

I love your preordained design
And am ready to play this role.
But the play being acted is not mine.
For this once let me go.

But the order of the acts is planned,
The end of the road already revealed.
Alone among the Pharisees I stand.
Life is not a stroll across a field.

1946   [JS/PF]

The Wind

I am dead, but you are living.
And the wind, moaning and grieving,
Rocks the house and the forest,
Not one pine after another
But further than the furthest
Horizon all together,
Like boat-hulls and bowsprits
In an unruffled anchorage,
Rocked not from high spirits
Or out of aimless rage,

But with a sad heart seeking
Words for your cradle-song.

1953   [JS/PF]

Hops

Beneath the willow, wound round with ivy,
We take cover form the worst
Of the storm, with a greatcoat round
Our shoulders and my hands around your waist.

I've got it wrong. That isn't ivy
Entwined in the bushes round
The wood, but hops. You intoxicate me!
Let's spread the greatcoat on the ground.

1953   [JS/PF]

Autumn

I have let my household disperse,
My dear ones have long been apart,
And a familiar loneliness
Fills all of nature and all my heart.

Here I am with you in the lodge.
No one walks through the woods these days.
As in the old song, undergrowth
Has almost hidden the forest ways.

Forlornly, the timber walls
Look down on the two of us here.
We did not promise to leap obstacles,
We shall fall at last in the clear.

We shall sit down from one till three,
You with embroidery, I deep
In a book, and at dawn shall not see
When we kiss each other to sleep.

More richly and more recklessly,
Leaves, leaves, give tongue and whirl away,
Fill yesterday's cup of bitterness
With the sadness of today.

Impulse, enchantment, beauty!
Let's dissolve in September wind
And enter the rustle of autumn!
Be still, or go out of your mind!

As the coppice lets slip its leaves,
You let your dress slip rustling down
And throw yourself into my arms
In your silk-tasselled dressing gown.

You are my joy on the brink
Of disaster, when life becomes
A plague, and beauty is daring,
And draws us into each other's arms.

c. 1947   [JS/PF]

Winter Night

Snow, snow, all the world over,
Snow to the world's end swirling,
A candle was burning on the table,
A candle burning.

As midges swarming in summer
Fly to the candle flame,
The snowflakes swarming outside
Flew at the window frame.

The blizzard etched on the window
Frosty patterning.
A candle was burning on the table,
A candle burning.

The lighted ceiling carried
A shadow frieze:

Entwining hands, entwining feet,
Entwining destinies.

And two little shoes dropped,
Thud, from the mattress.
And candle wax like tears dropped
On an empty dress.

And all was lost in a tunnel
Of grey snow churning.
A candle was burning on the table,
A candle burning.

And when a draught flattened the flame,
Temptation blazed
And like a fiery angel raised
Two cross-shaped wings.

All February the snow fell
And sometimes till morning
A candle was burning on the table,
A candle burning.

1948   [JS/PF]

Magdalene

Each night brings back my demon,
My fee for services rendered.
The memories of sin crowd in
Like vampires sucking at my heart,
Remembering how I surrendered
To men's desires, a crazy tart
Only at home on the boulevard.

A few minutes more and then
The lips of the grave will meet.
But first I will go as far
As I can, and break open
My life, Lord, at Your feet
Like an alabaster jar.

Oh, where now would I be,
My Teacher and Redeemer,
If every night eternity
Were not ensconced in my flat
And waiting like a customer,
Entangled in my net?

But what is the meaning of sin and death
And hell, when everyone can see
Me grafted indissolubly
To You, as a cutting to a tree,
In my immeasurable grief?

And, Jesus, when I press
Your feet against my knees,
Perhaps I am learning already
To hug the square shaft of a cross
And, swooning, I prepare Your body
For other oils than these.

1949   [JS/PF]

'In everything I want to reach'

In everything I want to reach
The very essence:
In work, in seeking a way,
In passion's turbulence.

The essence of past days
And where they start,
Foundations, roots,
The very heart.

Always catching the thread
Of actions, histories,
To live, to think, to feel, to love
To make discoveries.

If only I could do it
After a fashion,

I should compose eight lines
On the properties of passion,

On lawlessnesses, sins,
Pursuits, alarms,
On unexpectednesses,
Elbows, palms.

I should deduce its principles,
Its laws proclaim,
Repeating the initials
Of name after name.

I should plant out my stanzas.
And flowering limes,
Their veins astir with sap,
Would bloom in lines.

I should have mint and roses
Breathing there –
Sedge, meadows, haymaking,
And thunderous air.

So Chopin once enclosed
The plenitude
Of farmsteads, parks, groves, graves
In his *Etudes*.

The torment and delight
Of triumph so
Achieved tightens the bowstring
Bending the bow.

1956   [JS/PF]

Nobel Prize

Like a beast in a pen, I'm cut off
From my friends, freedom, the sun,
But the hunters are gaining ground.
I've nowhere else to run.

Dark wood and the bank of a pond,
Trunk of a fallen tree.
There's no way forward, no way back.
It's all up with me.

Am I gangster or murderer?
Of what crime do I stand
Condemned? I made the whole world weep
At the beauty of my land.

Even so, one step from my grave,
I believe that cruelty, spite,
The powers of darkness will in time
Be crushed by the spirit of light.

The beaters in a ring close in
With the wrong prey in view.
I've nobody at my right hand,
Nobody faithful and true.

And with such a noose on my throat
I should like for one second
My tears to be wiped away
By someone at my right hand.

1959   [JS/PF]

EVGENY VINOKUROV   1925–

Eyes

Exploded. To the ground. On his back. Arms apart. He
Raised himself to his knees, and bit his lips.
Across his face were smeared not tears
But eyes shot out.

Awful, awful. Bent double, I heaved
Him to one side. He was all
Covered with clay. I could hardly
Drag him across to the village.

In the field-hospital he cried
To the nurse: 'Oh it hurts! When you change
The bandage it's hell!' And I gave him, as one does,
Something to smoke as he lay dying.

And when, (taking him away) the wheels began
To whimper sharply, over all the voices
I suddenly remembered, for the first time:
My friend had pale blue eyes.

[AR]

'I do not like the circus'

I do not like the circus:
                              over there
Some of the people are chewing, and the others
Are sitting in their coats,
                              while straining every
Nerve the girl turns perfect somersaults
In the heights, among the lamps, half naked.

I cannot bear the beach:
                              this man makes jokes;
That one sprawls under canvas, looks out yawning
As a woman goes into the chilly sea,

Her golden edges glittering with blue.

I get cross at the movies.
                              This chap's drunk
And that one sleeps. The people chatter, giggle
Fearfully. And a woman fills the whole
Screen with her unclothed sacred body.

                        [AR]

Missing the Troop Train

There's something desperate about trains . . .
I stood alone on the icy platform,
Lost in the Bashkir steppes.
What can be more fantastic, more desolate
Than the light of an electric lamp
Rocking in a small station at night?
Trains swept past from time to time.
Their roar engulfed me,
I was submerged in coal dust,
And each time, I grabbed hold of my cap —
It looked as though I was greeting someone.
The bare, stunted tree by the side of the platform
Reached out after them . . .
I waited for one train at least
To stop, for God's sake!
In the distance was the dark forest mass.
I lifted my head —
Over me, a vast
Host of stars:
Regiments,
            divisions,
                        armies of stars,
All bound for somewhere.
An hour earlier, I'd got out of the train
To fetch some boiling water . . .
I could be court-martialled for this.
I stood there,

The snow melted round my boots,
And the water in the aluminium kettle I was holding
Had already iced over.
Above the forest mass, I saw
A little star,
Fallen a long way behind the others.
I looked at it
And it looked at me.

[DW]

Objects

I am deeply convinced that objects
Are more eloquent than words . . .

Here is the bell that summoned the weavers,
Furriers and tinsmiths to the *veche*.

Here is the bugle the Jacobins sounded
To herald the ending of the age of evil.

And here is the poker with which
They stirred the white ash in Auschwitz.

[DW]

The Stenographer

Twentieth century!
                        Fond of risks,
Life doesn't make it easy.
Stoic stenographer, you have
created the twentieth century.

Let the willows, weeping,
                        sorrow
over the elegiac pond, –
other mythologies grow
under your expeditious hand! . . .

So, instead of the chronicler,
                              a man
in cowl and cassock,
on high heels the muse came in
clasping a shorthand report.

        [DW]

ANDREI VOZNESENSKY   1933—

I Am Goya

I am Goya
of the bare field, by the enemy's beak gouged
till the craters of my eyes gape
I am grief

I am the tongue
of war, the embers of cities
on the snows of the year 1941
I am hunger

I am the gullet
of a woman hanged whose body like a bell
tolled over a blank square
I am Goya

O grapes of wrath!
I have hurled westward
                       the ashes of the uninvited guest!
and hammered stars into the unforgetting sky – like nails
I am Goya

    [sk]

First Frost

A girl is freezing in a telephone booth,
huddled in her flimsy coat,
her face stained by tears
and smeared with lipstick.

She breathes on her thin little fingers.
Fingers like ice. Glass beads in her ears.

She has to beat her way back alone
down the icy street.

First frost. A beginning of losses.
The first frost of telephone phrases.

It is the start of winter glittering on her cheek,
the first frost of having been hurt.

[SK]

Laziness

Blessed is laziness my sweet trap,
I'm too lazy to get up, or fall back to sleep.

Too lazy to get the phone. You reach out,
your waist touches my shoulder. You're all in,

your leg is over me. I listen
to your breath born like a bell in your throat.

'What tickets?' To hell with them. This slow-
ness of days, within us, turns to shadow.

Progress is laziness:
the key to Diogenes is laziness!

You are too good to be true. What I know
is laziness. The world is impossible. Let it go.

Too lazy to get the cable: 'push it under.'
Too lazy to eat, or end the sentence: today is Sund . . .

June has flopped down here,
drunk in the middle of the road,
like a goat-legged satyr
barefoot and in shorts.

[SM]

NATALYA GORBANEVSKAYA   1936–

'Why talk of disaster or beauty'

Why talk of disaster or beauty
when the oblivious body, happy,
naked as the thief's upon the cross,
wants to be deceived.

Who is it weeps and cries over me like a crane
crossing the snow line,
where the winter wind, the icy wind,
chills the bright surface of a well.

And this transcendental merging of passions,
these clutching hands, this gasping breath,
are like bones breaking softly on the cross
and, at the stake, the crackle and the blaze.

[DW]

'Nothing at all happens'

Nothing at all happens – neither fear,
nor stiffening before the executioner:
I let my head fall on the hollowed block,
as on a casual lover's shoulder.

Roll, curly head, over the planed boards,
don't get a splinter in your parted lips:
the boards bruise your temples,
the solemn fanfare sounds in your ears,

the polished copper dazzles the eyes,
the horses' mantle toss, –
O, what a day to die on!

Another day dawns sunless,
and in the twilight, half awake, or suffering
from some old fever or some new apocrypha,

my casual lover's shoulder
still smells to me of pine shavings.

[DW]

'The cricket sings on Twelfth-night'

The cricket sings on Twelfth-night,
on a January monday,
and the ringing of the bells
floats among the snow hills,
barely, barely touching
their silhouettes with its wing.

On Twelfth-night the cricket sings,
my chance visitor is silent,
and the ringing of the bells
drowns in the deep snow,
melts in the high sky,
in space that is cornerless.

But, in the corner by the stove,
like homunculi, the crickets
chirp, while all around
the ringing melts, and drowns,
but touches, in departing,
brushes us with its wing.

[DW]

'Outskirts of hostile towns'

Outskirts of hostile towns,
where the Roman alphabet rules the hoardings,
where Gothic contorts itself on the rooftops,
where the tramlines run straight down to the sea, –
oh stranger from afar, breathe in the air
of the outskirts just once, and you are ready,
open to meet the narrow windows,
and translucent, like roofs damp

after rain, and your whole face
radiant, like the tramway turn-table.

[DW]

'Here, as in a painting, noon burns yellow'

Here, as in a painting, noon burns yellow,
and the very air, like grief, is disembodied,
and in the utter silence, like a winged army,
the crows in Crow Park hang overhead.

But the mouldering leaves of years past
cling to my elbows, to my hands reeking
of cigarette smoke, and the bare shrubbery thrusts
its arms among my tangled curls.

I have left home so far behind me,
like a plane that in dense fog wanders
from the aerodrome into the darkness . . .
Am I living or dead, am I leaves or grass?

[DW]

'In my own twentieth century'

In my own twentieth century
where there are more dead than graves
to put them in, my miserable,
forever unshared love

among these Goya images
is nervous, faint, absurd,
as, after the screaming of jets,
the trump of Jericho.

[DW]

'And the hills are desolate, the valleys wild'

And the hills are desolate, the valleys wild,
the misty bridge is dim,
and the white tacks of the stars at dawn
are hammered into the sky.

On the edge of the land,
in the window a curtain flutters
like tidings of summer, like a summons
to strawberry picking.

And the red specks on the white skin
of my cheek
dry in the midday heat.
And dusk comes up from behind the hills,
pale, weightless,
like lorries floating into the mist.

[DW]

JOSEPH BRODSKY   1940–

'You're coming home again'

You're coming home again. What does that mean?
Can there be anyone here who still needs you,
who would still want to count you as his friend?
You're home, you've bought sweet wine to drink with supper,

and, staring out the window, bit by bit
you come to see that *you're* the one who's guilty:
the only one. That's fine. Thank God for that.
Or maybe one should say, 'Thanks for small favors.'

It's fine that there is no one else to blame,
it's fine that you are free of all connections,
it's fine that in this world there is no one
who feels obliged to love you to distraction.

It's fine that no one ever took your arm
and saw you to the door on a dark evening,
it's fine to walk, alone, in this vast world
toward home from the tumultuous railroad station.

It's fine to catch yourself, while rushing home,
mouthing a phrase that's something less than candid;
you're suddenly aware that your own soul
is very slow to take in what has happened.

1961   [GK]

from Elegy for John Donne

John Donne has sunk in sleep . . . All things beside
are sleeping too: walls, bed, and floor – all sleep.
The table, pictures, carpets, hooks and bolts,
clothes-closets, cupboards, candles, curtains – all
now sleep: the washbowl, bottle, tumbler, bread,
breadknife and china, crystal, pots and pans,
bed-sheets and nightlamp, chests of drawers, a clock,

a mirror, stairway, doors. Night everywhere,
night in all things: in corners, in men's eyes,
in bed-sheets, in the papers on a desk,
in the worm-eaten words of sterile speech,
in logs and fire-tongs, in the blackened coals
of a dead fireplace – in each thing.
In undershirts, boots, stockings, shadows, shades
behind the mirror; in the backs of chairs,
in bed and washbowl, in the crucifix,
in linen, in the broom beside the door,
in slippers. All these things have sunk in sleep.
Yes, all things sleep. The window. Snow beyond.
A roof-slope, whiter than a tablecloth,
the roof's high ridge. A neighborhood in snow,
carved to the quick by this sharp windowframe.
Arches and walls and windows – all asleep.
Wood paving-blocks, stone cobbles, gardens, grills.
No light will flare, no turning wheel will creak . . .
Chains, walled enclosures, ornaments and curbs.
Doors with their rings, knobs, hooks are all asleep –
their locks and bars, their bolts and cunning keys.
One hears no whisper, rustle, thump, or thud.
Only the snow creaks. All men sleep. Dawn comes
not soon. All jails and locks have lapsed in sleep.
The iron weights in the fish-shop are asleep.
The carcasses of pigs sleep too. Backyards
and houses. Watch-dogs in their chains lie cold.
In cellars sleeping cats hold up their ears.
Mice sleep, and men. And London soundly sleeps.
A schooner nods at anchor. The salt sea
talks in its sleep with snows beneath her hull,
and melts into the distant sleeping sky.
John Donne has sunk in sleep, with him the sea.
Chalk cliffs now tower in sleep above the sands.
This island sleeps, embraced by lonely dreams,
and every garden now is triple-barred.
Pines, maples, birches, firs, and spruce – all sleep.
On mountain slopes steep mountain-streams and paths
now sleep. Foxes and wolves. Bears in their dens.

The snow drifts high at burrow-entrances.
All the birds sleep. Their songs are heard no more.
Nor is the crow's hoarse *caw*. At night the owl's
dark hollow laugh is quenched. The open fields
of England now are stilled. A clear star flames.
The mice are penitent. All creatures sleep.
The dead lie calmly in their graves and dream.
The living, in the oceans of their gowns,
sleep – each alone – within their beds. Or two
by two. Hills, woods, and rivers sleep. All birds
and beasts now sleep – nature alive and dead.
But still the snow spins white from the black sky.
There, high above men's heads, all are asleep.
The angels sleep. Saints – to their saintly shame –
have quite forgotten this our anxious world.
Dark Hell-fires sleep, and glorious Paradise.
No one goes forth from home at this bleak hour.
Even God has gone to sleep. Earth is estranged.
Eyes do not see, and ears perceive no sound.
The Devil sleeps. Harsh enmity has fallen
asleep with him on snowy English fields.
All horsemen sleep. And the Archangel, with
his trumpet. Horses, softly swaying, sleep.
And all the cherubim, in one great host
embracing, doze beneath St Paul's high dome.
John Donne has sunk in sleep. His verses sleep.
His images, his rhymes, and his strong lines
fade out of view. Anxiety and sin,
alike grown slack, sleep in his syllables.
And each verse whispers to its next of kin,
'Move on a bit.' But each stands so remote
from Heaven's Gates, so poor, so pure and dense,
that all seems one. All are asleep. The vault
austere of iambs soars in sleep. Like guards,
the trochees stand and nod to left and right.
The vision of Lethean waters sleeps.
The poet's fame sleeps soundly at its side.
All trials, all sufferings, are sunk in sleep.
And vices sleep. Good lies in Evil's arms.

The prophets sleep. The bleaching snow seeks out,
through endless space, the last unwhitened spot.
All things have lapsed in sleep. The swarms of books,
the streams of words, cloaked in oblivion's ice,
sleep soundly. Every speech, each speech's truth,
is sleeping. Linked chains, sleeping, scarcely clank.
All soundly sleep: the saints, the Devil, God.
Their wicked and their faithful servants. Snow
alone sifts, rustling, on the darkened roads.
And there are no more sounds in all the world . . .

[GK]

A Slice of Honeymoon
to M.B.

Never, never forget:
how the waves lashed the docks,
and the wind pressed upward
like submerged life-buoys.

– How the seagulls chattered,
sailboats stared at the sky.
– How the clouds swooped upwards
like wild ducks flying.

May this tiny fragment
of the life we then shared
beat in your heart wildly
like a fish not yet dead.

May the bushes bristle.
May the oysters snap.
May the passion cresting
at your lips make you grasp

– without words – how the surf
of these breaking waves
brings fresh crests to birth
in the open sea.

1963   [GK]

Aeneas and Dido

The great man stared out through the open window;
but her entire world ended at the border
of his broad Grecian tunic, whose abundance
of folds had the fixed, frozen look of seawaves
long since immobilized.
                              And still he stared
through the wide window with a gaze so distant
that his lips seemed to freeze and form a seashell,
one that concealed an inward, muted roar.
The shimmering horizon in his goblet
was motionless.
                              But her vast love appeared
to be only a fish, a fish which yet
might plunge into the sea after his ship,
knifing the waves with its slim supple body,
and somehow overtake him – except that he,
in thought, already strode upon dry land.
The sea became a sea of shining tears.
But, as we know, precisely at the moment
when our despair is deepest, fresh winds stir.
The great man sailed from Carthage.
                              Dido stood
alone before the bonfire which her soldiers
had kindled by the city walls, and there –
as in a vision trembling between flame
and smoke – she watched great Carthage silently
crumble to ash,

long ages before Cato's prophecy.

1969   [GK]

May 24, 1980

I have braved, for want of wild beasts, steel cages,
carved my term and nickname on bunks and rafters,
lived by the sea, flashed aces in an oasis,

dined with the-devil-knows-whom, in tails, on truffles.
From the height of a glacier I beheld half a world, the earthly
width. Twice have drowned, thrice let knives rake my nitty-gritty.
Quit the country that bore and nursed me.
Those who forgot me would make a city.
I have waded the steppes that saw yelling Huns in saddles,
worn the clothes nowadays back in fashion in every quarter,
planted rye, tarred the roofs of pigsties and stables,
guzzled everything save dry water.
I've admitted the sentries' third eye into my wet and foul
dreams. Munched the bread of exile: it's stale and warty.
Granted my lungs all sounds except the howl;
switched to a whisper. Now I am forty.
What should I say about life? That it's long and abhors
    transparence.
Broken eggs make me grieve; the omelette, though, makes me vomit.
Yet until brown clay has been crammed down my larynx,
only gratitude will be gushing from it.

1980

A Martial Law Carol
to Wiktor Woroszylski and Andrzej Drawicz

One more Christmas ends
soaking stripes and stars.
All my Polish friends
are behind steel bars,
locked like zeroes in
some graph sheet of wrath:
as a discipline
slavery beats math.

Nations learn the rules
like a naughty boy
as the tyrant drools
manacles in joy.
One pen stroke apiece,
minus edits plus

helping the police
to subtract a class.

From a stubborn brow
something scarlet drops
on the Christmas snow.
As it turns, the globe's
face gets uglier,
pores becoming cells,
while the planets glare
coldly, like ourselves.

Hungry faces. Grime.
Squalor. Unabashed
courts distribute time
to the people crushed
not so much by tanks
or by submachine
guns as by the banks
we deposit in.

Deeper than the depth
of your thoughts or mine
is the sleep of death
in the Vujek mine;
higher than your rent
is that hand whose craft
keeps the other bent –
as though photographed.

Powerless is speech.
Still, it bests a tear
in attempts to reach,
crossing the frontier,
for the heavy hearts,
of my Polish friends.
One more trial starts.
One more Christmas ends.

1989

from A Part of Speech

I was born and grew up in the Baltic marshland
by zinc-gray breakers that always marched on
in twos. Hence all rhymes, hence that wan flat voice
that ripples between them like hair still moist,
if it ripples at all. Propped on a pallid elbow,
the helix picks out of them no sea rumble
but a clap of canvas, of shutters, of hands, a kettle
on the burner, boiling – lastly, the seagull's metal
cry. What keeps hearts from falseness in this flat region
is that there is nowhere to hide and plenty of room for vision.
Only sound needs echo and dreads its lack.
A glance is accustomed to no glance back.

*

The North buckles metal, glass it won't harm;
teaches the throat to say, 'Let me in.'
I was raised by the cold that, to warm my palm,
gathered my fingers around a pen.

Freezing, I see the red sun that sets
behind oceans, and there is no soul
in sight. Either my heel slips on ice, or the globe itself
arches sharply under my sole.

And in my throat, where a boring tale
or tea, or laughter should be the norm,
snow grows all the louder and 'Farewell!'
darkens like Scott wrapped in a polar storm.

Stone Villages

The stone-built villages of England.
A cathedral bottled in a pub window.
Cows dispersed across the fields.
Monuments to kings.

A man in a moth-eaten suit
sees a train off, heading, like everything here, for the sea,

smiles at his daughter, leaving for the East.
A whistle blows.

And the endless sky over the tiles
grows bluer as swelling birdsong fills.
And the clearer the song is heard,
the smaller the bird.

1976   [AM]

TRANSLATORS

Translators are listed here (in alphabetical order of surname) against the initials that stand at the foot of the poems they have translated. Where more than one translator has the same initials, the poet whose work is translated by each is given in brackets.

AA	A. Alvarez	ML	Michael Longley
AB	Anne Born	RL	Richard Lourie
BC	Bo Carpelan		(Aleksander Wat)
JC/BC	John and Bogdana Carpenter	RL	Robert Lowell (Eugenio Montale)
DC	David Constantine	GM	George MacBeth
CC	Cid Cornan	DM	Derek Mahon
PC	Patrick Creagh	JM	James Merrill
MC	Margaret Crosland		(Eugenio Montale)
JC	János Csokits	JM/IM	Jarmila and Ian Milner
AC	Adam Czerniawski	CM	Czeslaw Milosz
ME	Maurice English	EM	Edwin Morgan
DJE	D. J. Enright	SM	Stanley Moss
RF	Ruth Feldman (Primo Levi)	PM	Paul Muldoon
		AM	Alan Myers
PF	Peter France	LN	Leonard Nathan
RF	Robin Fulton (Tomas Tranströmer)	EO	Ewald Osers
		AP	Alfredo de Palchi (Eugenio Montale)
RG	Renata Gorczynski	AP	Anne Pennington
MH	Michael Hamburger		(Vasko Popa)
SH	Seamus Heaney (Marin Sorescu)	SR	Sonia Raiziss
AH	Anselm Hollo	GR	George Rapp
SH	Stuart Hood (Erich Fried)	VR	Vinio Rossi
		JR	Jerome Rothenberg
TH	Ted Hughes	AR	Anthony Rudolf
GK	George Kline	IRG	Ioanna Russell-Gebbett
SK	Stanley Kunitz	PS	Peter Dale Scott
HL	Herbert Lomas	GS	Gaia Servadio

JS	Jon Stallworthy	DW	David Wevill
NS	Nikos Stangos		(Ferenc Juhász)
BS	Brian Swann	CW/GG	Clive Wilmer and
GT	George Theiner		George Gömöri
DW	Daniel Weissbort	CW	Charles Wright
	(Evgeny Vinokurov,		(Eugenio Montale)
	Natalya	DY	David Young
	Gorbanevskaya)		

ACKNOWLEDGEMENTS

For permission to reprint copyright material the publishers gratefully
acknowledge the following:

INGEBORG BACHMANN: 'To the Sun' (1956, *Anrufen des grossen
Baren*), 'Fog Land' (1956), 'Every Day' (1957, *Die Gestundete Zeit*),
'The Respite' (1957, *Die Gestundete Zeit*) and 'Exile' (1964, *Gedichte,
Erzahlungen, Hotspiel, Essays*) translated by Michael Hamburger, by
permission of Michael Hamburger

ANTONÍN BARTUŠEK: 'Exile from Paradise','Simonetta Vespucci',
'Snapshot from a Family Outing', 'The Return of the Poets' and
'Epitaph', translated by Ewald Osers, by permission of Ewald Osers

JOSEPH BRODSKY: 'You're coming home again', *from* 'Elegy for John
Donne', 'A Slice of Honeymoon' and 'Aeneas and Dido' from *Selected
Poems*, translated by George L. Kline (Penguin Books, 1973),
translation copyright © George L. Kline, 1973; 'May 24, 1980' and 'A
Martial Law Carol' from *To Urania: Selected Poems 1965–1985* by
Joseph Brodsky (Penguin Books, 1988), by permission of Penguin
Books Ltd; *from* 'A Part of Speech' and 'Stone Villages' from *A Part of
Speech* by Joseph Brodsky (OUP, 1980), by permission of Oxford
University Press

BO CARPELAN: 'At Grand Opera', 'Removal vans drew children like
ambulances', 'You had to watch out', 'For a moment they stand out',
'When you drive up to the four-star pump' and 'Old Man', from *Room
Without Walls: Selected Poems by Bo Carpelan*, translated by Anne
Born (Forest Books, 1987), by permission of Forest Books; 'Address'
from *Paint the Sky: Poems for little and big people* (*Maia himlen. Vers
for sma och stora*, 1988), translated by Herbert Lomas, by permission
of Herbert Lomas; 'Here is a field with spring dew', 'As we started on
our way up', 'The bees that increase and diminish' and 'Mile after mile
the roots go', translated by Robin Fulton, by permission of Robin
Fulton

PAUL CELAN: 'Death Fugue', 'Think of it', 'Psalm', 'Tenebrae',
'Homecoming', 'Time's Eye', 'Nocturnally Pouting', 'Your hand full of
hours', 'Sand from the Urns', 'Aspen tree, your leaves glance white',
'Memory of France' and 'Corona', translated by Michael Hamburger,
by permission of Michael Hamburger

HANS MAGNUS ENZENSBERGER: 'for the grave of a peace-loving man', 'Visiting Ingres', 'The Divorce', 'The Force of Habit' and 'Concert of Wishes', translated by Michael Hamburger, by permission of Michael Hamburger

ERICH FRIED: 'Death Certificate' (1969), translated by George Rapp; 'Transformation', 'Conservation of Matter', 'What Happens', 'Premonition of Final Victory' and 'Old Salts', translated by Stuart Hood, from *One Hundred Poems without a Country* by Erich Fried, translated by Stuart Hood (John Calder, 1978, reprinted 1990), copyright © Eric Fried 1969, 1978 and 1990, by permission of the Erich Fried Estate and Calder Publications Ltd, London; 'The Measures Taken' and 'Unoccupied Room' translated by Michael Hamburger, by permission of Michael Hamburger

NATALYA GORBANEVSKAYA: 'Why talk of disaster or beauty', 'Nothing at all happens', 'The cricket sings on Twelfth-night', 'Outskirts of hostile towns', 'Here, as in a painting, noon burns yellow', 'In my own twentieth century' and 'And the hills are desolate, the valleys wild' from *Selected Poems*, edited by Daniel Weissbort (Carcanet Press, 1972), by permission of Carcanet Press Limited

PAAVO HAAVIKKO: *from* 'The Short Year', *from* 'Poems from the House of a Novgorod Merchant', *from* 'In the World' ('I vote for spring', 'The best of man', 'When the bad lady', 'In debt for goose eggs' and 'The seedlings the firs need'), and *from* 'May, Perpetual' from *Contemporary Finnish Poetry*, translated by Herbert Lomas (Bloodaxe Books, 1991), by permission of Bloodaxe Books Ltd; *from* 'Ten Poems from the Year 1966' and *from* 'In the World' ('I have seen eyes', 'The world has always been a terrible place' and 'This is a world') from *Selected Poems*, translated by Anselm Hollo (Carcanet Press, 1991), copyright © 1991 Paavo Haavikko (poems) and Anselm Hollo (translations), by permission of Carcanet Press Limited

ZBIGNIEW HERBERT: 'Two Drops', 'Arion', 'A Knocker', 'Maturity', 'Rosy Ear', 'Silk of a Soul', 'Parable of the Russian Emigrés', 'Episode in a Library', 'The Wind and the Rose', 'Hen', 'Pebble' and 'Why the Classics' from *Selected Poems*, translated by Czeslaw Milosz and Peter Dale Scott (Penguin Books, 1968), translation copyright © Czeslaw Milosz and Peter Dale Scott, 1968, by permission of Penguin Books Ltd; 'What Mr Cogito Thinks about Hell' and 'The Envoy of Mr Cogito' from *Selected Poems*, translated by John and Bogdana Carpenter (OUP, 1977), © John and Bogdana Carpenter 1977, and

'Mr Cogito Thinks of Returning to the City Where he Was Born' from
Mr Cogito: Poems by Zbigniew Herbert, translated by John and
Bogdana Carpenter (OUP, forthcoming 1993), by permission of
Oxford University Press

VLADIMÍR HOLAN: 'Human Voice', 'Daybreak', 'Meeting in a Lift',
'Deep in the Night', 'Snow', 'Verses', 'Reminiscence II', 'Ubi nullus
ordo, sed perpetuus horror', 'After St Martin's Day II', 'Fourth
Month', 'Glimpsed', 'Dream', 'During an Illness', 'Twelfth Night',
'Goodbye' and 'For Himself' from *Selected Poems*, translated by
Jarmila and Ian Milner (Penguin Books, 1971), copyright © Vladimir
Holan, translations copyright © Jarmila and Ian Milner, 1971, by
permission of Penguin Books Ltd

MIROSLAV HOLUB: 'In the Microscope', 'Polonius', 'Love', 'A Boy's
Head', 'Reality', 'Pathology', 'Death in the Evening', 'Five Minutes
after the Air Raid', 'The Fly', 'Wings', 'A Helping Hand', 'Žito the
Magician', 'Suffering', 'The Prague of Jan Palach', 'Alphabet', 'The
Dead' and 'Half a Hedgehog' from *Poems Before & After* (collected
English translations), translated by Ian and Jarmila Milner, Ewald
Osers and George Theiner (Bloodaxe Books, 1990), by permission of
Bloodaxe Books Ltd

PHILIPPE JACCOTTET: 'Ignorance', 'Distances', 'End of Winter', 'Each
flower is a little night', 'Grapes and figs', 'Who will help me?', 'It's easy
to talk', 'Quick write this book', 'I rise with an effort', 'Glimpses' and
'To Henry Purcell' from *Selected Poems*, translated by Derek Mahon
(Viking, 1988), poems copyright © Philippe Jaccottet, 1957, 1967,
1969, 1974, 1983, by permission of Penguin Books Ltd

TYMOTEUSZ KARPOWICZ: 'Lesson in Silence', 'False Alarm', 'Dream'
and 'Ecclesiastes' from *The Burning Forest: New Polish Poetry*,
translated by Adam Czerniawski (Bloodaxe Books, 1988) by
permission of Bloodaxe Books Ltd; 'The Pencil's Dream' from *Postwar
Polish Poetry*, edited by Czeslaw Milosz, translation copyright 1965 by
Czeslaw Milosz, by permission of Doubleday, a division of Bantam
Doubleday Dell Publishing Group, Inc

PRIMO LEVI: 'Reveille', 'The Gulls of Settimo', 'The Survivor', 'The
Elephant' and 'Sidereus Nuncius' from *Collected Poems*, translated by
Ruth Feldman and Brian Swann (Faber, new edition, 1992), by
permission of Faber and Faber Limited; 'The Opus', translated by Gaia
Servadio and A. Alvarez, by permission of A. Alvarez

CZESLAW MILOSZ: 'Dedication', 'Mid-twentieth-century Portrait', 'Gift',

'Secretaries', 'After Paradise', 'Winter', 'Preparation', 'A Portrait with a
Cat' and 'And yet the Books' from *The Collected Poems 1931–1987*
(Viking, 1988), copyright © Czeslaw Milosz Royalties, Inc, 1988, by
permission of Penguin Books Ltd

EUGENIO MONTALE: 'The Storm', 'In Sleep', 'The Strands of Hair', 'To
My Mother', 'Ballad Written in a Clinic', 'In the Greenhouse', 'The
Hitler Spring', 'The Shadow of the Magnolia', 'The Eel' and 'Little
Testament' from *Selected Poems* (New Directions, 1965), copyright ©
1965 by New Directions Publishing Corporation, by permission of
New Directions Publishing Corporation

BORIS PASTERNAK: 'Hamlet', 'The Wind', 'Hops', 'Autumn', 'Winter
Night', 'Magdalene', 'In everything I want to reach' and 'Nobel Prize'
from *Selected Poems*, translated by Jon Stallworthy and Peter France
(Allen Lane, 1983), copyright © Peter France, 1983, by permission of
Penguin Books Ltd

CESARE PAVESE: 'Death shall come, using your eyes' and 'I shall go
through the Piazza di Spagna' from *Selected Poems*, translated by
Margaret Crosland (Penguin Books, 1971) by permission of Peter
Owen Ltd

GYÖRGY PETRI: 'I am stuck, Lord, on your hook', 'Apocryphal', 'On the
24th Anniversary of the Little October Revolution', 'Night Song of the
Personal Shadow', 'To Imre Nagy', 'Cold Peace' and 'Morning Coffee'
from *Night Song of The Personal Shadow: Selected Poems*, translated
by Clive Wilmer and George Gomori (Bloodaxe Books, 1991), by
permission of Bloodaxe Books Ltd

JÁNOS PILINSZKY: 'Harbach 1944', 'The French Prisoner', 'On the Wall
of a KZ-Lager', 'Passion of Ravensbrück', 'Impromptu', 'Straight
Labyrinth' and 'Jewel' from *The Desert of Love*, translated by János
Csokits and Ted Hughes (Anvil Press, 1989), by permission of Anvil
Press Poetry Ltd

FRANCIS PONGE: 'The Wasp-woman', translated by George MacBeth,
from *George MacBeth: Collected Poems, 1958–1982* (Hutchinson,
1989), by permission of Sheil Land Associates Ltd

VASKO POPA: 'Pig', 'Before Play', 'The Nail', 'The Seducer', 'The Rose
Thieves', 'He', 'The Hunter', 'Ashes', 'Black be your tongue', 'I've
wiped your face off my face', 'Preparations for a Welcome' and
'Midnight Sun', from *Complete Poems*, translated by Anne
Pennington, revised and expanded by Francis R. Jones (Anvil Press,
forthcoming 1993), by permission of Anvil Press Poetry Ltd

YANNIS RITSOS: 'Morning', 'Almost a Conjuror', 'The Suspect',
   'Approximately', 'Submission', 'First Pleasure', 'The Potter', 'After the
   Defeat', 'Penelope's Despair' and 'Search' from *Selected Poems*,
   translated by Nikos Stangos (Penguin Books, 1974), by permission of
   Nikos Stangos
TADEUSZ RÓŻEWICZ: 'The Survivor', 'Living Star', 'A Visit', 'Chestnut',
   'Abattoirs', 'But whoever sees', 'What Luck', 'Pigtail', 'Massacre of the
   Boys', 'The Colour of her Eyes and Questions', 'Who's Absent', 'Leave
   Us', 'Posthumous Rehabilitation', 'A Meeting', 'To the Heart', 'They
   Shed the Load', 'Leda', 'Draft for a Contemporary Love Poem',
   'Proofs', 'In the Theatre of Shades' and 'I was sitting in an easy-chair'
   from *They Came To See a Poet*, translated by Adam Czerniawski
   (Anvil Press, 1991), by permission of Anvil Press Poetry Ltd
MARIN SORESCU: 'Destiny', 'Precautions', 'Cure', 'Sealess', 'Adam', 'The
   Compass', 'The Tear', 'Evolution' and 'Fountains in the Sea' from *The
   Biggest Egg in the World* translated by Ioanna Russell-Gebbett with
   Seamus Heaney, Ted Hughes, David Constantine, D. J. Enright,
   Michael Hamburger, Michael Longley, Paul Muldoon and William
   Scammell (Bloodaxe Books, 1987); 'Leda', 'The Complaint' and 'The
   Actors' from *Selected Poems*, translated by Michael Hamburger
   (Bloodaxe Books, 1983), by permission of Bloodaxe Books Ltd
TOMAS TRANSTRÖMER: 'Morning Approach', 'Tracks', 'Winter's
   Formulae', 'Alone', 'A Few Minutes' and 'To Friends behind a
   Frontier' from *Collected Poems*, translated by Robin Fulton (Bloodaxe
   Books, 1987), by permission of Bloodaxe Books Ltd
GIUSEPPE UNGARETTI: 'Day by Day', 'Bitter Chiming', 'You Were
   Broken', 'In My Veins', 'Cry Out No More' and 'Variations on
   Nothing' from *Selected Poems*, translated by Patrick Creagh (Penguin
   Books, 1971), translation copyright © Patrick Creagh, 1971, by
   permission of Penguin Books Ltd
EVGENY VINOKUROV: 'Eyes', 'I do not like the circus', 'Missing the
   Troop Train', 'Objects' and 'The Stenographer', from *The War Is
   Over*, translated by Anthony Rudolf and Daniel Weissbort (Carcanet
   Press, 1976), by permission of Carcanet Press Limited
ALEKSANDER WAT: 'To Be a Mouse', 'Arithmetic', 'A Flamingo's
   Dream', 'Imagerie d'Epinal', 'From Persian Parables', 'From Notes
   Written in Obory', 'Childhood of a Poet', 'Japanese Archery', 'A Joke',
   'To a Roman, my Friend', 'Taking a Walk', 'To Leopold Labedz' and
   'The Bride' from *Selected Poems*, translated and edited by Czeslaw

Milosz and Leonard Nathan (Penguin Books, 1991), copyright ©
Aleksander Wat, translation copyright © Czeslaw Milosz and Leonard
Nathan, 1969, by permission of Penguin Books Ltd
SÁNDOR WEÖRES: 'The Colonnade of Teeth', 'Orpheus Killed', 'Terra
Sigillata', 'In Memoriam Gyula Juhász', 'The Secret Country' and
'Monkeyland' from *Selected Poems of Sándor Weöres* (translated by
Edwin Morgan) *and Ferenc Juhasz* (translated by David Wevill)
(Penguin Books, 1970), by permission of Edwin Morgan
ADAM ZAGAJEWSKI: 'Late Beethoven', 'A River', 'Good Friday in the
Tunnels of the Métro' and 'In the Encyclopedias, No Room for Osip
Mendelstam', from *Tremor: Selected Poems*, translated by Renata
Gorczynski (Collins Harvill, 1987), by permission of HarperCollins
Publishers Limited

Faber and Faber Limited apologize for any errors or omissions in the
above list and would be grateful to be notified of any corrections that
should be incorporated in the next edition or reprint of this volume.